D1171528

What Can I Do Now?

Art

Books in the
What Can I Do Now? Series

Art
Computers
Engineering, Second Edition
Fashion
Health Care
Music
Nursing, Second Edition
Radio and Television, Second Edition
Safety and Security, Second Edition
Sports, Second Edition

What Can I Do Now?

Art

Ferguson Publishing

An imprint of Infobase Publishing

What Can I Do Now? Art

Copyright © 2007 by Infobase Publishing

All rights reserved. No part of this book may be reproduced or utilized in any form or by any means, electronic or mechanical, including photocopying, recording, or by any information storage or retrieval systems, without permission in writing from the publisher. For information contact:

Ferguson
An imprint of Infobase Publishing
132 West 31st Street
New York NY 10001

ISBN-10: 0-8160-6025-8
ISBN-13: 978-0-8160-6025-2

Library of Congress Cataloging-in-Publication Data
What can I do now? Art.
    p. cm.
    Includes index.
    ISBN 0–8160–6025–8 (hc : alk. paper)
    1. Art—Vocational guidance—United States—Juvenile literature. I. Title: Art.
    N6505.W48 2007
    702.3—dc22   2006028878

Ferguson books are available at special discounts when purchased in bulk quantities for businesses, associations, institutions, or sales promotions. Please call our Special Sales Department in New York at (212) 967-8800 or (800) 322-8755.

You can find Ferguson on the World Wide Web at http://www.fergpubco.com

Text design by Kerry Casey
Cover design by Takeshi Takahashi

Printed in the United States of America

VB FOF 10 9 8 7 6 5 4 3 2 1

This book is printed on acid-free paper.

All links and Web addresses were checked and verified to be correct at the time of publication. Because of the dynamic nature of the Web, some addresses and links may have changed since publication and may no longer be valid.

Contents

Introduction

If you're considering a career in art—which presumably you are since you're reading this book—you must realize that the better informed you are from the start, the better your chances of having a successful, satisfying career.

There is absolutely no reason to wait until you get out of high school to "get serious" about a career. This doesn't mean you have to make a firm, undying commitment right now. Indeed, one of the biggest fears most people face at some point (sometimes more than once) is choosing the right career. Frankly, many people don't "choose" at all. They take a job because they need one, and all of a sudden 10 years have passed and they wonder why they're stuck doing something they hate. Don't be one of those people! You have the opportunity right now—while you're still in high school and still relatively unencumbered with major adult responsibilities—to explore, to experience, to try out a work path—or several paths if you're one of those overachieving types. Wouldn't you really rather find out sooner than later that you're not as interested in art therapy as you thought? That maybe you'd prefer to be an art teacher, or a painter, or an art gallery owner?

There are many ways to explore the art industry. What we've tried to do in this book is give you an idea of some of your options. Section 1, "What Do I Need to Know about Art," will give you an overview of the field—a little history, where it's at today, and promises of the future, as well as a breakdown of the structure of the field (how it's organized) and a glimpse of some of its many career options.

Section 2, "Careers," includes 10 chapters, each describing in detail a specific art career—art conservators, art dealers, art teachers, art therapists, ceramic artists, gallery directors, illustrators, multimedia artists, painters, and photographers. The educational requirements for these specialties range from high school diploma to graduate degree. These chapters rely heavily on firsthand accounts from real people on the job. They'll tell you what skills you need, what personal qualities you have to have, and what the ups and downs of the jobs are. You'll also find out about educational requirements—including specific high school and college classes—advancement possibilities, salary ranges, and the future outlook.

In keeping with the secondary theme of this book (the primary theme, as you might have guessed, is "You can do something now"), Section 3, "Do It Yourself," urges you to take charge and start your own programs and activities where none exist—whether at school, in your community, or nationally.

1

The real meat of the book is in Section 4, "What Can I Do Right Now?" This is where you get busy and *do something*. The chapter "Get Involved" outlines the obvious volunteer and intern positions and the not-so-obvious summer camps and summer college study, as well as student art organizations.

"Read a Book" is an annotated bibliography of books (some new, some old) and periodicals. If you're even remotely considering a career in art, reading a few books and checking out a few magazines is the easiest thing you can do. Don't stop with our list. Ask your librarian to point you to more art materials. Keep reading!

While many think the best way to explore art is to jump right in and start doing it, there are plenty of other ways to get into the art mind-set. The chapter "Surf the Web" offers you a short annotated list of art Web sites where you can explore everything from job listings (start getting an idea of what employers are looking for now) to educational requirements to overviews of art movements and profiles of famous artists.

"Ask for Money" is a sampling of art scholarships and other types of financial aid. You need to be familiar with these because you're going to need money for school. You have to actively pursue scholarships; no one is going to come up to you in the hall one day and present you with a check because you're such a wonderful student or a great artist. Applying for scholarships is work. It takes effort. And it must be done right and often a year in advance of when you need the money.

"Look to the Pros" is the final chapter. It contains a list of professional organizations that you can turn to for more information about accredited schools, education requirements, career descriptions, salary information, job listings, scholarships, and much more. Once you become an art student, you'll be able to join many of these groups. Time after time, professionals say that membership and active participation in a professional organization is one of the best ways to network (make valuable contacts) and gain recognition in your field.

High school can be a lot of fun. There are dances and football games; maybe you're in band or play a sport. These are all good things. Then again, maybe you hate school and are just biding your time until you graduate. Whoever you are, take a minute and try to imagine your life five years from now. Ten years from now. Where will you be? What will you be doing? Whether you realize it or not, how you choose to spend your time now—studying, playing, watching TV, working at a fast food restaurant, hanging out, whatever—will have an impact on your future. Take a look at how you're spending your time now and ask yourself, "Where is this getting me?" If you can't come up with an answer, the answer is probably "nowhere." The choice is yours. No one is going to take you by the hand and lead you in the "right" direction. It's up to you. It's your life. You can do something about your future right now.

SECTION 1

What Do I Need to Know about Art?

Georgia O'Keefe's painting *Black Iris,* Michelangelo's sculpture *David,* and Robert Mapplethorpe's photograph *Fish* all express the diversity of the visual arts. Today, visual arts include not only the traditional fields of painting, drawing, and sculpture, but also illustration, photography, filmmaking, needlework, even computer animation, as well as many others. Works of art are wonderful to look at, and they enhance our lives and help us understand ourselves and our societies. They inspire us, comfort us, touch us, and heal us. They reflect our imagination and excite our vision.

This exciting field offers a diverse range of careers from the artists who actually create works of art; to the professionals who preserve, exhibit, and sell art; to the educators who teach us about art and the health care professionals who use art to heal the mentally and physically ill. In short, opportunities in art are only limited by your imagination.

GENERAL INFORMATION

Many of the visual arts created by humans have their origins in prehistoric times, and we know by looking at artifacts that the visual arts have been important in virtually every human society. World cultures offer an abundance of styles and media in the visual arts.

The earliest examples of Western painting are found not on the walls of elegant museums but on the walls of caves in southern Europe. Famous ancient cave art is found at Lascaux in southwestern France and Altamira in northern Spain.

It is believed that some 20,000 years ago, humans painted pictures of animals such as bison, horses, and deer on cave walls as part of magic rituals to benefit their hunting trips. Scientists have determined that their paint was made of various minerals mixed with animal fat, egg whites, plant juices, fish glue, or blood, and the first paintbrushes were made of twigs and reeds. Prehistoric sculpture is represented by small animal figures and fertility statuettes, such as the Venus of Willendorf. These are found from Eastern Europe to Siberia but mainly in Austria, the Czech Republic, and Hungary.

Egyptians around 3000 B.C. used visual art to honor their pharaohs. They painted the walls of their tombs with mythological figures and depictions of everyday activities, such as hunting, fishing, and banquets. Minoans (ancestors of the Greeks) of the 1500s B.C. left paintings on the walls of palaces in Crete and on pottery. The Romans adopted many Greek artistic techniques, decorating their floors with mosaics and creating wall frescoes that portrayed rituals, myths, landscapes, and scenes of daily life.

In the thousands of years since the ancient Romans and Greeks, some aspects of the visual arts have remained constant while others have changed. In wealthy societies certain classes of people are able to pay professional artists, as Sumerian priests and Renaissance princes did, and as art collectors and corporations do today.

The physical resources of a society have always affected the medium in which an artist works. In Mesopotamia, Sumerian architects built with brick because stone was not available. Nomadic Asian herders wove wool from their flocks into rugs. Medieval European painters worked on wood panels, plaster walls, and stained-glass windows, and calligraphers drew letters on parchment in an era before paper was known in the West. Because of mass production and world trade, 20th-century artists have an enormous range of materials from which to choose. Today, anything goes—artists create works not only with paint and paper but with metals, glass, fabric, even household appliances.

Local tradition also affects art styles. Pottery design in one area and period may be geometric; in another, naturalistic. Because of Indian traditions, artists depicted the Buddha with tightly curled hair. Western tradition decreed that the Madonna be shown with a blue robe. Eastern artists seem to have disregarded scientific perspective, which was a major concern of painters in the European Renaissance. In ancient Egyptian culture, which was dominated by the state and religion, painting, sculpture, and architecture glorified the pharaoh and life after death. In pious medieval Europe, most visual arts had Christian themes. In 20th-century totalitarian countries, art served the state. In most Western countries, artists have great freedom to choose the subjects that they desire.

Art movements, or schools of thought, are numerous: impressionism, postimpres-

Modern Art Movements

Impressionism: This painting movement began in mid-19th century France with artists Monet, Renoir, Pissarro, Degas, Morisot, Cezanne (in his early years), and the American painter Cassatt. These artists worked from life, mostly out-of-doors. Impressionism sometimes describes the technique of breaking up the picture surface into small dabs of broken color that would be blended together by the viewer's eye.

Post-Impressionism: This type of painting followed Impressionism in France, and included the work of artists such as Cezanne, Gauguin, Seurat, and Van Gogh. It was less naturalistic than Impressionism and led to the notion of painting as essentially colors and forms on a flat surface.

Symbolism: Symbolism began in the 1890s in Europe and was influenced by Art Nouveau and Post-Impressionism. Symbolist artists included Redon, Bonnard, and Vuillard.

Fauvism: This movement emphasized bright colors and shapes not conforming to objective reality; includes the art of Matisse and Derain.

Cubism: Cubism began in France with Picasso and Braque, who were inspired by African sculpture and Cezanne's paintings. It was characterized by images shown as geometrical shapes and the use of multiple perspectives. Other artists included Gris and Feininger.

(continued on next page)

(continued from previous page)

Abstraction: Abstract art modifies or distorts objective reality. Some of the first abstractionists were Kandinsky and Mondrian.

Dada: Dadaism included the work of Marcel Duchamp. It tried to shock, defy conventions, and question the very definitions of art.

Surrealism: Surrealistic painters, such as Dali, Miro, Ernst, and Magritte, experimented with the ideas of the subconscious and dreams in art, the importance of the element of chance, and the concept of an absolute in art.

Abstract Expressionism: Abstract Expressionism began mainly in America in the 1940s, with the work of Pollock, Newman, and Rothko. Common elements included a spiritual nature of the work, the elements of chance and the unconscious, and the absence or distortion of objective reality.

Expressionism: Expressionism is sometimes considered the German version of Fauvism. It focuses on the expression of emotion, rather than a description of physical reality. Kirchner and Nolde were Expressionists.

Pop Art: Pop artists made art that separated the artist's personality from the work, in contrast to Expressionism. Images were often taken from advertising and the contemporary world. Pop Art's early artists were Rauschenberg, Johns, and Warhol.

Op Art: Op art was a strictly visual exploration of colors and other optical effects in painting. Artists included Vasarely and Albers.

Earth or Environmental Art: Environmental artists use the natural world as its material and content. Christo and Jeanne-Claude are the best-known environmental artists. Their art explores concepts and often has poetic and art-for-all qualities.

Conceptual Art: Conceptual art emphasizes the idea of the work of art as opposed to the object itself. It can be an act done by an artist or a physical object made by the artist. Hamilton and Boltanski are conceptual artists who explore ideas about the nature of reality.

Installation Art: Installation art describes very large, usually three-dimensional collections of objects and forms, often filling a large gallery or museum space. Examples of Installation artists are Kienholz, Segal, and Pfaff.

sionism, expressionism, surrealism, cubism, dadaism, fauvism, futurism, abstract expressionism, and minimalism are just a few. Although these movements change with time and space, visual art continues to be a power that confronts us, challenges us, and allows us to comment on life in expressive ways.

STRUCTURE OF THE INDUSTRY

The visual arts are roughly divided into three categories: commercial art, fine art, and craft. Commercial art is art used by advertising, publishing, public relations, and other business enterprises to attract attention, sell products and services, illustrate concepts, convey messages, and document events. Some commercial art, particularly certain types of illustration and photography, is also considered by some to be fine art. Most commercial art combines pictorial elements with text, and artists use a variety of media to create primarily two-dimensional works that can be easily reproduced. Computers are an important tool commercial artists use to design page layouts, specify type fonts and sizes, scan photos and artwork, separate colors for printing, create illustrations, and manipulate photos.

Fine art is art created more for personal expression than financial gain. Although some fine artists are commissioned to create works for a particular place, such as a park or an office building, usually the art comes from the artist's own ideas. The list of materials fine artists use to create their art is inexhaustible. They use paint, clay, metal, wood, stone, papier mâché, plastic, ink, pencil, paper, wood, charcoal, fabric, computers, and other materials to create art.

Only a few fine artists make a living from their art. Most earn income from other occupations while making art in their free time. The most common way for fine artists to show and sell their art is through galleries. Galleries hold single-artist shows, group shows, theme shows, and competitions. They also represent specific artists and act as art brokers between artists and buyers. Artists assemble a portfolio of slides of their most representative work and present it to gallery owners and directors. When gallery owners and directors consider representing an artist, they look at the artist's body of work. They like to see a progression of concept or technique and to know that the artist is likely to continue producing quality work. After a work or works are accepted for exhibit, they are installed in the gallery. There is usually an opening reception, to which interested viewers, critics, and potential buyers are invited to meet and talk with the artist. The installation or exhibit may be open for public viewing for a week or several months. Fine artists also display their art in public buildings, restaurants, museums, office buildings, hotels, and on the Internet. In fact, fine artists are using the Internet more and more to make their works visible and available to a much wider audience than is possible by galleries and other exhibiting venues.

The field of visual arts also includes craft, sometimes called handcraft, or arts and crafts. Craft refers to art objects that usually, but not always, have a function. Needle arts, jewelry making, basketry, wood carving, mosaic, some ceramics, and bookbinding are examples of crafts, although there is some disagreement about what is craft and what is fine art. Crafters sell their works through retail stores, fairs, catalogs, the Internet, and galleries.

In addition to artists who actually create and market works of art, there are a wide variety of other workers—such as art teachers, historians, appraisers, curators, therapists, and writers—who play an important role in the industry. See Section 2, "Careers," for a further discussion of specific art careers.

Glossary

calligraphy Writing with artistic, stylized, or elegant lettering; the art of producing such lettering.

collage Art composed of a variety of materials, such as paper, cloth, wood, and metal, glued to a surface.

etching The art of producing pictures or designs by printing from a metal plate that has been etched with a substance like acid or a laser beam.

masterpiece A work of art done with extraordinary skill; a supreme artistic achievement.

medium The material an artist chooses to work in, such as marble, oil paint, and ink.

mixed media More than one type of medium (like paint, thread, and metal) used to create a work of art.

needlework Handcraft involving fabrics, such as embroidery, knitting, crocheting, needlepoint, quilting, lace making, and weaving.

potter An artist who forms clay into earthenware objects and figures. Sometimes known as a ceramic artist, ceramist, sculptor, and clay artist.

printmaking Making an original work of art (like a woodcut, etching, or lithograph) that is intended to be graphically reproduced.

sculpture A three-dimensional work of art.

watercolors Paints made of pigment and water dispersed in a binding material.

CAREERS

The following paragraphs describe some of the most prominent art careers.

- *Archivists* identify, preserve, and catalog historical documents and works of art for those who are writing about, researching, or teaching art.
- *Art appraisers* determine the authenticity and value of works of art, including paintings, sculptures, and antiques. They examine works for color values, brushstroke style, and other characteristics to establish the piece's age or to identify the artist. Art appraisers are well versed in art history, art materials, techniques of individual artists, and contemporary art markets, and they use that knowledge to assign values. Art appraisers may use complex methods such as X-rays and chemical tests to detect fraud.
- *Art conservators* preserve and restore aged, faded, or damaged art. They also evaluate the age and authenticity of the work. Restoring art can be tedious and detailed work, requiring the precise and skillful application of solvents and cleaning agents to the work. Art conservators also repair damaged sculpture, pottery, jewelry, fabrics, and other items, depending on their area of expertise.
- *Art dealers* acquire, display, and sell art and antiques. They may own their own galleries, rent space at an antique or art mall, or sell art solely on the Internet.
- *Art directors* play a key role in every stage of the creation of an advertisement or ad campaign, from formulating concepts to supervising

Employment for Selected Workers in the Arts, 2003

Career	Employment
Art Directors	24,790
College Art, Drama, and Music Teachers	62,010
Commercial and Industrial Designers	32,940
Fine Artists (including Painters, Sculptors, and Illustrators)	9,370
Multi-Media Artists and Animators	32,030
Photographers (includes commercial photographers)	56,210

Source: U.S. Department of Labor

production. Ultimately, they are responsible for planning and overseeing the presentation of their clients' messages in print or on screen—that is, in books, magazines, newspapers, television commercials, posters, and packaging, as well as in film and video and on the Internet.

- *Art historians* gather, interpret, and evaluate works of art and records of the past in order to describe and analyze past events, institutions, ideas, movements, and people (including artists). Skill in research and writing is essential to their work, but scientific methods are also invaluable.

- *Art librarians* perform many of the same duties as traditional librarians, but specialize in managing materials related to art. They are employed at art museums, large research libraries, colleges and universities, public libraries, art foundations, and publishing companies.

- *Art museum curators* oversee the maintenance, preservation, archiving, cataloging, study, and display of collection components. Curators may fund-raise to support staff in the physical care and study of collections. They also add to or alter a museum's collection by trading objects with other museums or purchasing new pieces. They educate others through scholarly articles and public programs that showcase the items. Curators also are employed by special libraries and historical societies.

- *Art museum directors* are responsible for the daily operations of the museum, for long-term planning, policies, any research conducted within the museum, and for the museum's fiscal health. Directors must also represent the museum at meetings with other museums, business and civic communities, and the museum's governing body. Finally, art museum directors ensure that museums adhere to state and federal guidelines for safety in the workplace and hiring practices, as well as industry recommendations concerning the acquisitions and care of objects within the museum.

- *Art photographers* use photography as a vehicle for artistic expression. The work of art photographers is collected by those with a special interest in the field, shown in galleries, and displayed in museums of art. The work of well-known photographers in this field is often collected and published in book form. There is some overlap between this and other forms of photography. The work of some photographers who did not set out to create works of art is nevertheless considered to have great artistic value. This category can include portraiture and photojournalism, as well as landscape, nature, architecture, and still life photography.
- *Art teachers* educate students of all ages about art techniques, history, movements, and other art-related subjects.
- *Art therapists* use the creative processes of art to treat and rehabilitate people with mental, physical, and emotional disabilities.
- *Art writers* write articles and books about artists, art movements, exhibitions at galleries and museums, and other art-related topics. They work for newspaper, magazine, and book publishers or may be self-employed.
- *Cartoonists* are illustrators who draw pictures and cartoons to amuse, educate, and persuade people. They work for newspapers, magazines, cartoon syndicates, book publishers, and advertising agencies. Some are self-employed.
- *Ceramic artists* use clay and glazes to create sculpture, tableware, beads, tiles, or architectural decorations. They are also known as *potters, ceramists, sculptors,* and *clay artists.*
- *Fiber artists* create wall hangings and sculpture from textiles, threads, and paper.
- *Furniture designers* are commercial artists who develop concepts for building furnishings like chairs, tables, and couches. They work closely with their clients to get a thorough understanding of what kind of product is needed.
- *Glass workers,* including *stained glass artists, glassblowers,* and *etchers,* work with glass to create art. Stained glass artists cut colored pieces of glass, arrange them in a design, and connect them with leading. The leading is then soldered to hold the glass pieces together. Glassblowers use a variety of instruments to blow molten glass into bottles, vases, and sculptures. Etchers use fine hand and power tools, and sometimes chemicals, to create a design in the surface of glass.
- *Graphic designers* are commercial artists whose creations are intended to express ideas, convey information, or draw attention to a product. They design a wide variety of materials including advertisements, displays, packaging, signs, computer graphics and games, book and magazine covers and interiors, animated characters, and company logos to fit the needs and preferences of their various clients.

- *Gallery directors* manage every aspect of an art gallery—including marketing, sales, acquisitions, working with staff and artists, and financial issues.
- *Gallery owners* own and operate art galleries. They handle the business side of selling art, such as marketing and promotion, and arranging purchases, in return for a percentage of any money received.
- *Illustrators* are commercial artists (although some illustrators create fine art) who prepare drawings for advertisements, magazines, books, newspapers, packaging, Web sites, computer programs, and other formats. *Medical illustrators,* who have special training in biology and the physical sciences, are able to draw accurate illustrations of parts of the human body, animals, and plants. *Fashion illustrators* specialize in distinctive illustrations of the latest women's and men's fashions.
- *Jewelry designers* conceive and sketch ideas for jewelry that they may make themselves or have made by another craftsperson. The materials they use may be precious, semiprecious, or synthetic. They work with valuable stones such as diamonds and rubies, and precious metals such as gold, silver, and platinum. Some jewelry designers use synthetic stones in their jewelry to make items more affordable.
- *Multimedia artists* incorporate several techniques, such as painting, sculpture, collage, printing, computer technology, and drawing, into one work of art.
- *Painters* paint a variety of subjects, such as landscapes, people, or objects. They work with oil paint, acrylic paint, tempera, watercolors, gouache, pen and ink, or pastels, but they may also incorporate such nontraditional media as clay, paper, cloth, and a variety of other material. They use brushes, palette knives, airbrushes, and other tools to apply color to canvas, paper, or other surfaces. Painters use line, texture, color, and other visual elements to produce the desired effect.
- *Printmakers* engrave, etch, or mask designs on wood, stone, metal, or silk screen. These designs are then transferred, or printed, on paper. Printmakers can also create their art using computers. These artists use computer scanners to scan the prepared plates and then reproduce prints using high-quality color printers.
- *Sculptors* use materials such as clay, metal, wood, stone, papier mâché and plastic to build, carve, sandblast, cast, or mold three-dimensional forms.
- *Silversmiths* design, assemble, decorate, or repair silver articles. They may specialize in one or more areas of the jewelry field such as repairing, selling, or appraising.

EMPLOYMENT OPPORTUNITIES

According to the U.S. Department of Labor, there are approximately 149,000 artists in the United States—with hundreds of thousands of additional workers employed as art educators, therapists,

Top Master of Fine Arts Programs

1. Rhode Island School of Design (http://www.risd.edu)
2. School of the Art Institute of Chicago (http://www.artic.edu/saic)
3. Yale University (http://www.yale.edu/art)
4. California Institute of the Arts (http://www.calarts.edu)
5. Cranbrook Academy of Art (http://www.cranbrook.edu)

Source: *U.S. News & World Report,* 2003

conservators, appraisers, consultants, gallery owners and directors, and in other occupations. Art is such a broad field that there are literally countless places where you can find employment, depending on your specialty.

There is no magic formula for success in the visual arts. Often, luck and innate skill and talent are important as training. Competition is high, even for positions in the non-artistic areas related to the field such as gallery owners and directors, art therapists, and art writers. In general, most creative art positions are part time. Many visual artists hold down jobs outside of the arts to support themselves. Most artists are self-employed and earn money according to their ability to sell their work. Many visual artists combine their artistic work with careers as teachers and professors of art. They may give private lessons, lead workshops, or be employed at art schools, colleges and universities, and other places where art instruction is given. Some visual artists such as photographers may focus on both fine and commercial art to pay the bills. Others artists may own a gallery and show their work and the work of others to make a living. Visual artists may pursue additional education to become art appraisers, conservators, therapists, or journalists.

INDUSTRY OUTLOOK

As long as the visual arts continue to be an outlet for creative expression, people with artistic skills and dreams will continue to work in this field. The large number of art exhibits, galleries, and Web sites will continue to offer employment opportunities to skilled visual artists. However, those who aspire to a career in this field should recognize that although the possibilities of success exist and can be fulfilling, the potential for disappointment is also real. Fine artists and crafters often find it difficult to support themselves financially by their artwork alone. The visual arts are a highly subjective area, and success depends a lot on the aesthetic perceptions and choices of the audiences who view works of art.

However, even with heavy competition and different opinions of beauty, according to the *Occupational Outlook Handbook,* it is expected that employment of visual artists will grow as fast as the average for all occupations through 2014. The industry will grow in proportion to its ability to attract audiences. Also, the growth of the Internet will create lots of opportunities for all artists. Chances for artists to exhibit their work often depend on the amount of government funding available. The National Endowment for the Arts and local arts agencies offer various financial grants to artists, for which competition is heavy.

SECTION 2

Careers

Art Conservators

SUMMARY

Definition
Art conservators carry out conservation treatments and programs on works of art.

Alternative Job Titles
Art restorers
Conservation workers

Salary Range
$19,720 to $34,090 to $60,180+

Educational Requirements
Bachelor's degree

Certification or Licensing
None available

Employment Outlook
About as fast as the average

High School Subjects
Art
Chemistry

Personal Interests
Art
Fixing things
Science

Steven Erisoty was busy restoring a painting in his studio when the phone rang. The call was from the curator of the Biggs Museum of American Art in Dover, Delaware, who asked if he had time to conserve two portraits of Brandt Schuler and Margareta Van Wyck Schuler painted by John Wollaston in 1750. The museum's founder had purchased the rare paintings in what turned out to be his last gift to the museum before his death. The museum wanted to have the portraits conserved in time for its 10th anniversary celebration that fall.

When the curator brought the paintings to Steven's studio, they discovered some very disturbing condition problems.

"Both paintings had discolored varnish layers and had been heavily restored in the early 20th century," Steven recalls. "The portrait of Brandt Schuler had multiple areas of repaint, but much original paint remained intact and it would be a time-consuming, but straightforward, treatment. The portrait of Margareta Van Wyck Schuler was another matter entirely. Her face had been so heavily repainted that she no longer looked like a portrait by Wollaston, and a past cleaning had heavily abraded her pearl necklace and lace cap. This would be a real challenge."

Steven took detailed photographs of the paintings, wrote condition reports,

16

and began the treatment. "The removal of the discolored varnish layers revealed just how much repaint was covering the portrait of Mrs. Schuler," he explains. "Then, while viewing the paint surface through a binocular microscope, the repaints were painstakingly removed with a variety of cleaning agents and scalpels. The image revealed had been heavily damaged by a previous cleaning attempt. There were many areas of missing paint, but at least now it looked like a Wollaston. Her cheeks were narrower and her lips less full, and the formerly flat expanses of color on her face were now gently shaded to give contours and form to the image. Careful inpainting of the paint losses, without covering original paint, brought back the wise, gentle expression that Wollaston had captured on her face. But still, the question of the original appearance of the severely damaged lace cap and necklace remained. Upon close inspection, there were indications of what each area should look like, but such a judgment had to be an educated one."

Steven asked the curator to locate photos of other paintings by Wollaston where he had painted pearls and lace. "By combining what visible evidence was left with images of intact Wollaston pearls and lace," Steven says, "it was possible to reconstruct the damaged areas in a way that Wollaston could have painted them."

Steven's conservation work was a success, and the Biggs Museum could now proudly display its patron's last bequest during its anniversary celebration.

WHAT DOES AN ART CONSERVATOR DO?

Art conservators, or *art restorers,* analyze and assess the condition of artifacts and pieces of art, plan for the care of art collections, and carry out conservation treatments and programs. Conservators may be in private practice or work for museums, historical societies, or state institutions. When conserving artifacts or artwork, these professionals must select methods and materials that preserve and retain the original integrity of each piece. Art conservators must be knowledgeable about the objects in their care, such as paintings, sculpture, paper, and metal.

Art conservators generally choose to specialize in one type of artwork, such as the preservation of books and paper, objects, photographic materials, paintings, or wooden artifacts. There are also conservators who specialize in archaeology or ethnographic materials. Many are employed by museums, while others provide services through private practice. Conservation activities include carrying out technical and scientific studies on art objects, stabilizing and restoring the appearance of the work, and establishing the environment in which the art is best preserved. A conservator's responsibilities also may include documenting the structure and condition of the piece through written and visual recording, designing programs for preventive care, and executing conservation treatments. Conservation tools include organic solvents that remove dirt and other debris, microscopes, cameras, and equipment for specialized processes such as infrared and ultraviolet photography and X-rays.

Before working on a piece of art, conservators study descriptions and information about the object, such as the materials used and the period during which it was created. Only after extensive research and consideration does the conservator begin work. Even then, the conservator works slowly and cautiously, performing chemical and physical tests on small areas of the work so as not to damage the original piece.

Paintings are slowly and meticulously restored using solvents and cotton swabs. If an object is metal, an art conservator might clean it by scraping or by applying chemical solvents. Statues are washed with soap solutions, and furniture and silver is polished.

When a repair is necessary, conservators reassemble the broken pieces using glue or solder (a metallic substance used to join metal surfaces), then buff the object when the repair is complete. They also inpaint areas where the original paint is missing, making sure to use paint that is a different chemical composition than the original (this allows for reversability in restoration and stability as the new paint ages).

Conservation work may be conducted indoors, in laboratories, or in an outdoor setting. Conservators typically work 40 to 60 hours per week depending on exhibit schedules and deadlines, as well as the amount and condition of unstable objects in their collections. Because some conservation tasks and techniques involve the use of toxic chemicals, laboratories are equipped with ventilation systems. At times a conservator may find it necessary to wear a mask and possibly even a respirator when working with particularly harsh chemicals or varnishes. Most of the work requires meticulous attention to detail, a great deal of precision, and manual dexterity.

A *conservation scientist* is a professional scientist whose primary focus is in developing materials and knowledge to support conservation activities. Some specialize in scientific research into artists' materials, such as paints and varnishes. *Conservation educators* have substantial knowledge and experience in the theory and practice of conservation and have chosen to direct their efforts toward teaching the principles, methodology, and technical aspects of the profession. *Preparators* supervise the installation of specimens, art objects, and artifacts, often working with design technicians, curators, and directors to ensure the safety and preservation of items on display.

The rewards of the conservation profession are the satisfaction of preserving works of art that reflect the diversity of human achievements; being in regular contact with art; enjoying a stimulating workplace; and the creative application of expertise to the preservation of artistically and historically significant objects.

WHAT IS IT LIKE TO BE AN ART CONSERVATOR?

Steven Erisoty has been an art conservator since 1983. "A career in art conservation is a stimulating lifetime of problem solving," he says. "It is very satisfying to be able to—through structural stabilization, cleaning, repaint removal, and careful inpainting of damages—reveal an artist's message so that it can be appreciated by the viewer again. Sometimes very fine artworks have become so damaged that the average person can no longer see the value in the object. Giving that image back to the world is very rewarding. It is also very satisfying to help people preserve and enjoy their cherished possessions, regardless of whether the object has any monetary value or not." (Visit http://www.artconservators alliance.com to learn more about Steven and his associates' work as art conservators and to see a photo of him at work restoring a painting.)

Steven's typical day involves meeting with clients; writing condition or treatment reports; taking photos before, during, or after treatment; structural repairs; cleaning, inpainting, and revarnishing; and ordering or picking up materials. His primary responsibility, he says, is the ethical care, preservation, and restoration of art objects. "All art, in fact, all material things, change as they age. When an artist creates a work of art, he or she is presenting a specific message or set of ideas to the viewer. As that artwork ages, it may change in visual appearance. For example, paint may develop cracks, pigments can fade, and the support or canvas may become weak and distorted. In addition, misguided attempts to repair damages by well-meaning amateurs can further alter the appearance of an artwork. Each change that alters the appearance of an artwork pushes that artwork further and further away from the artist's original message to the viewer, until sometimes that message becomes so obscured that it is lost. The goal of an art conservator is to interfere as little as possible, in order to preserve and reveal as much of the artist's message as possible."

Steven's secondary responsibility as an art conservator is to educate the owners of artwork about the ethical treatment and care of art objects, so that they will be able to best preserve their treasures for future generations. "It can sometimes be frustrating when you are not able to convince people to give their object the best care," he says. "It amazes me that some owners of artwork, which they supposedly value, can be penny wise and pound foolish. It is our job to educate them about all the steps needed to do quality

To Be a Successful Art Conservator, You Should . . .

- have the ability to concentrate for long periods of time during conservation work
- be attentive to detail
- have good manual dexterity
- love art in all its forms
- have patience to work on restoration projects that may last months or even years

work. Once people understand how long proper conservation takes to do, they are in general willing to have you do it."

DO I HAVE WHAT IT TAKES TO BE AN ART CONSERVATOR?

Conservation work can be physically demanding. Art conservators need to be able to concentrate on specific physical and mental tasks for long periods of time. Attention to detail is crucial. Endurance, manual dexterity, and patience are often needed to complete projects successfully. Work on one piece of art could take months or even years; because of the fragile nature of the materials, conservation work should never be rushed.

Finally, an important personal quality to have for this line of work is a respect and love for art. Conservators should appreciate the value in all art forms (regardless of personal bias) and treat all pieces that they work on with the utmost care.

HOW DO I BECOME AN ART CONSERVATOR?

Steven first heard about the career of art conservation as a high school student. "Since I was so interested in the arts," he says, "I had been given a school day to spend in a museum, with a curator, so that I might learn about the various job options in museums. As I helped the curator with some chores, he asked me about my interests and hobbies. I told him about my interest in art, that I liked to

Related Jobs

- archivists
- art appraisers
- art dealers
- art historians
- ceramic artists
- conservation administrators
- conservation technicians
- curators
- fine arts packers
- jewelers and jewelry repairers
- multimedia artists
- museum technicians
- painters
- preservation specialists
- sculptors

restore antique furniture and cane chair seats. He said to me, 'Well, you ought to be a conservator!' Having never heard the term before I asked him what one was. He then explained what a conservator did and that there were graduate programs in art conservation. He also told me that there was an undergraduate program at the University of Delaware set up with the proper courses to prepare an applicant for the graduate programs in art conservation." Steven applied, was accepted, and took the prescribed course of study, which at that time was an interdepartmental major in art history and chemistry, with a strong concentration in studio art. "After receiving my college degree," he says, "I applied to and was accepted into the Cooperstown Graduate Program in the Conservation of Historic and Artistic Works."

Education

High School

Good conservation work comes from a well-balanced formulation of art and science. To prepare for a career in conservation, concentrate on doing well in all academic subjects, including courses in chemistry, natural science, history, and the arts.

Postsecondary Training

In the past, many conservation professionals earned their training solely through apprenticeships with esteemed conservators. The same is not true today; you will need a master's degree to work as an art conservator. Steven agrees. "Naturally you want to be the very best at what you do," he says, "and it is very difficult to truly understand what you are doing without having had the proper courses in art, art history, and science. It is the difference between being able to follow a recipe and create one. Do not be afraid of the chemistry, art, or art history. Few people are naturally adept in all three areas. If you are passionate about preserving artworks for the future, you will get though the course work and find yourself an art conservator some day."

At the undergraduate level, take course work in the sciences, including inorganic and organic chemistry, the humanities (especially art history and anthropology), and studio art. Many graduate with degrees in art history, chemistry, or studio art.

If you do not go to a university that has an undergraduate program in art conservation, Steven advises that you should consult the graduate programs in art conservation about the courses necessary to take in college so that you are properly prepared. "You will need actual experience in the field in order to get accepted into a graduate program," he advises. "Try to find the time to do volunteer work in the conservation department of a local museum or with a qualified conservator, as soon as possible. This will also help you to decide if art conservation is a field that really interests you."

Graduate programs typically last three or four years, with the final year being an internship year. This final year involves working full time in a conservation specialty under the guidance of an experienced conservator. Steven feels that the course work in graduate school was challenging, but in a good way. "I had been well prepared by my undergraduate studies," he says, "and enjoyed my learning experiences in graduate school immensely." The American Institute for Conservation of Historic and Artistic Works offers links to educational programs at its Web site, http://aic.stanford.edu/education/becoming.

Internships and Volunteerships

Because employment in this field, even at entry level, most often entails the handling of precious materials and cultural resources, you should be fairly well prepared before contacting professionals to request either internship or volunteer positions. You need to demonstrate a high level of academic achievement and have a serious interest in the career to edge out the competition for a limited number of jobs.

Most often students entering the field of art conservation have completed high school and undergraduate studies, and many are contemplating graduate programs. At this point a student is ready to seek a position (often unpaid) as an apprentice or intern with either a private conservation company or a museum to gain a practical feel for the work. Training opportunities are scarce and in high demand. Prospective students must convince potential trainers of their dedication to the highly demanding craft of conservation. The combination of academic or formal training along with hands-on experience and apprenticeship is the ideal foundation for entering the career.

Contact professional organizations, such as the American Institute for Conservation of Historic and Artistic Works, for directories of internships, training, and conservation programs.

WHO WILL HIRE ME?

Steven's first job in the field was the internship he had in graduate school. He spent the final year of his graduate studies working in the Art Conservation Lab at the Philadelphia Museum of Art. "While there, I worked on paintings in the museum's collection," he says. "I was fortunate enough to work on paintings by Monet, Cezanne, Jan Steen, and Adrian van Ostade. I also gained experience in environmental monitoring, art condition surveys, and art packing."

After receiving his graduate degree, Steven continued to work for the museum as an assistance conservator. "When the funding for my position, which was not a permanent one, came to an end," he says, "curators at the museum put me in touch

---

Learn More about Conservation Education

The following U.S. and Canadian colleges and universities offer training in art conservation. Visit their Web sites for more information on conservation, recommended courses, and graduation requirements.

Columbia University (New York)
http://www.arch.columbia.edu

Harvard University Art Museums, Straus Center for Conservation (Cambridge, Mass.)
http://www.artmuseums.harvard.edu/straus

New York University (New York)
http://www.nyu.edu/gsas/dept/fineart/ifa/index_chan.htm

Queens University (Kingston, Canada)
http://qsilver.queensu.ca/arth/programs_artc.html

University of California-Los Angeles
http://ioa.ucla.edu/conservation

University of Delaware (Newark)
http://www.udel.edu/artcons

University of Pennsylvania (Philadelphia)
http://www.design.upenn.edu/new/hist

with a local collector of 17th-century Italian paintings. This collector had recently purchased several rather large, rare, but very damaged paintings, which needed delicate work to bring out their best qualities. This collector kept me employed virtually full time for several years while I slowly set up a private practice as an art conservator in Philadelphia."

Museums, libraries, historical societies, private conservation laboratories, and government agencies hire art conservators. Institutions with small operating budgets sometimes hire part-time specialists to perform conservation work. This is especially common when curators need extra help in preparing items for display. Antique dealers may also seek the expertise of an experienced art conservator for merchandise restoration, identification, and appraisal purposes.

WHERE CAN I GO FROM HERE?

Steven is very happy with the current size of his business. "I like doing the actual conservation work," he says. "It would be possible to expand and have a studio full of employees, but that would mean putting in a lot of time as an administrator, and that is not what I enjoy doing. I do enjoy coordinating mural projects outside the studio, and that involves employees and education of conservation students. It helps to feel like you are giving back to the field a bit. One goal of mine is to continue to educate the public about ethics and standards in conservation, so that

less and less poor quality work is found to be acceptable."

Due to rapid changes in each conservation specialty, practicing conservators must keep abreast with advances in technology and methodology. Conservators need to stay up-to-date. To keep current with developments in conservation, Steven is a member of the American Institute for Conservation of Historic and Artistic Works, reads publications, attends professional meetings, and enrolls in short-term workshops, courses, and seminars.

An experienced conservator wishing to move into another realm of the field may become a private consultant, an appraiser of art or artifacts, a conservation educator, a curator, or a museum registrar.

WHAT ARE THE SALARY RANGES?

Salaries for conservators vary greatly depending on the level of experience, chosen specialty, region, job description, and employer. The U.S. Department of Labor, which classifies conservators with curators, museum technicians, and archivists, reports the median annual earnings for this group as $34,090 in 2005. The lowest paid 10 percent of this group earned less than $19,720, and the highest paid 10 percent made more than $60,180.

According to the American Institute for Conservation of Historic and Artistic Works, a first-year conservator can expect to earn approximately $20,000 annually. Conservators with several years of experience report annual earnings between $35,000 and $40,000. Senior conservators have reported earnings between $50,000 and $60,000 annually.

Fringe benefits, including paid vacations, medical and dental insurance, sick leave, and retirement plans, vary according to each employer's policies.

WHAT IS THE JOB OUTLOOK?

The U.S. Department of Labor predicts the employment of art conservators will grow at an average rate through 2014. However, competition for these desirable positions, especially in museums, will be strong. "Employment in museums is limited," Steven says. "At this point the major museums have permanent conservation positions that become available upon the retirement of the current staff. People wanting to go into conservation will very likely be faced with opening a private studio in an area that is currently underserved by professionals with degrees. Currently there are still numerous people working as conservators who do not have degrees; their work can range from good to terrible. It is up to the next generation of educated conservators to continue to educate the public about what ethical conservation is, so that the standards of what the public expects, and the quality of the work performed, goes up in general."

The public's developing interest in cultural material of all forms will contribute to art conservation and preservation as a growing field. New specialties have emerged in response to the interest in collections maintenance and preventive care. Conservation, curatorial, and registration responsibilities are intermingling and creating hybrid conservation professional titles, such as collections care, environmental monitoring, and exhibits specialists.

Despite these developments, however, any decreases in federal funding often affect employment and educational opportunities. For example, in any given year, if Congress limits government assistance to the National Endowment for the Arts, less money is available to assist students through unpaid internships. As museums experience a tightening of federal funds, many may choose to decrease the number of paid conservators on staff and instead may rely on a small staff augmented by private conservation companies that can be contracted on a short-term basis as necessary. Private industry and for-profit companies will then continue to grow, while federally funded nonprofit museums may experience a reduction of staff.

Art Dealers

SUMMARY

Definition
Art dealers acquire, display, and sell art.

Alternative Job Titles
None

Salary Range
$12,000 to $30,000 to $100,000+

Educational Requirements
High school diploma

Certification or Licensing
None available

Employment Outlook
About as fast as the average

High School Subjects
Art
Business
Foreign language

Personal Interests
Art
Business management
Selling/making a deal
Travel

As an art dealer, Howard Rehs wears many hats. One minute he's a photographer, the next, a salesperson. Then he's designing and posting to Web sites for his business, then it's on to e-mailing, calling, instant messaging, and travel to auctions. And his work doesn't end when he leaves his gallery at 5:00 P.M. After a quick dinner with family, he's back in his home office taking calls from his clients who, for good or bad, have his home number.

items more than 100 years old, but often are commonly associated with art, as well as furniture, jewelry, clothing, and household goods.

People collect a wide array of art pieces, from traditional paintings and sculptures to pop-art items such as decorated cigar boxes and caricatures. Many art dealers are self-employed and go into business after discovering an interest in collecting pieces themselves.

WHAT DOES AN ART DEALER DO?

Art dealers make a living acquiring, displaying, and selling antique and modern art. Antiques are formally defined as

WHAT IS IT LIKE TO BE AN ART DEALER?

Howard Rehs is an art dealer and the owner (along with his father) of Rehs Galleries, Inc. (to learn more about the gallery, visit http://www.rehs.com) in New York City. It is one of the world's leading art galleries that specializes in 19th- and 20th-century French, British, and American paintings. "The business was founded by my grandfather back in the 1930s," Howard explains. "My father entered the business in the early 1960s, and I began working part time in the gallery during my teenage years. I love what I do and find very few negatives. I enjoy looking at fine works of art, talking with some of the most interesting people in the world, and meeting people from many different backgrounds working in diverse businesses."

Howard begins a typical work day at home around 8:30 A.M. by checking e-mails on his computer. After taking care of pressing business, he drives to his gallery. "After opening, I check phone messages and again any e-mail messages," he says. "I then verify the status of any shipments that were sent the prior day and make sure everything is on schedule for delivery. If there are any problems, I contact the shippers and follow up with clients."

Howard then makes any necessary updates to his gallery's Web site—he maintains it himself—as well as makes, or requests, changes to other sites in which his gallery is featured. "The Internet has enabled us to see works and buy them without ever leaving the gallery," Howard says.

"The balance of my day," he says, "is divided between dealing with individuals who may visit the gallery; talking with existing clients either by phone or through instant messaging (sometimes doing both at the same time); handling any advertising issues; photographing (both digitally and in 4 x 5 format) any works that have just arrived (I do all our photography); color correcting the digital images; printing any photos that need to be sent to clients who do not use the Internet; writing letters; sending out e-mail offerings; ordering frames for new works; coordinating the restoration pickup; packing any works that are to be shipped that day and preparing the shipping documents. Since we purchase many of our works privately, I also follow up with individuals who have offered us works. Additionally, we receive many auction catalogs from around the world. Those need to be looked at and, if there is something of interest, we contact the specific departments and ask for any additional information we require."

With the exception of purchasing expeditions, much of art dealers' time is spent at the gallery. Many smaller art galleries do not operate with a large staff, so dealers must be prepared to work alone at times. Also, there may be large gaps of time between customers. Time can be easily filled, though, as Rehs can attest to. When he's not with a client in his gallery, on the phone, e-mailing, or otherwise communicating with clients, Howard spends time researching the lives of the 19th-century artists Julien Dupré, Daniel Ridgway Knight, and Emile Munier for the gallery's catalogue raisonné (an annotated catalog of an artist's work). Additionally, as president of the Fine Art Dealers Association, he handles issues relating to that organization.

Most galleries are open at least five days a week and operate during regular business hours, though some have extended shopping hours in the evening. Owners of galleries typically work longer hours based on the fact they have to do all the tasks that a normal business owner has to do (payroll, budgeting for new acquisitions to the gallery, collecting payments) in addition to showing work. "While I do work long hours," Howard says, "they are far less stressful than my friends and clients who work in the medical, legal, and financial worlds."

Howard leaves the gallery between 5:00 and 5:30 P.M. each day. After dinner, he heads to his home office to check and respond to e-mails and phone messages. "As most of our clients have my home phone number," he says, "I do, at times, spend part of the evening talking with one or two of them."

Art dealers are not always stuck in their gallery. Buying trips and shopping expeditions give them opportunities to restock their inventory, not to mention explore different regions of the country or world. Howard makes purchasing trips and attends auctions in New York, other U.S. cities, and even Europe. "For many years I did travel quite a bit," he says, "mainly to Europe to buy paintings. However over the years we have found that many of the great works of art in the areas we deal in can be found in the United States. So now there is less of a need to travel to Europe."

DO I HAVE WHAT IT TAKES TO BE AN ART DEALER?

To be an art dealer, you'll need patience—and lots of it. Keeping your gallery well stocked takes numerous buying trips, as well as time surfing the Web. Unless you're lucky enough to have a large staff, you will have to conduct these searches yourself. However, most art dealers go into the profession because they enjoy the challenge of hunting for valuable pieces. "I enjoy the hunt for a new work, the acquisition of that work, and the ability to place it in the right collection," says Howard.

In addition to being patient in the hunt for treasure, art dealers also have to be patient when dealing with clients. Works of art can cost thousands, even millions of dollars; as a result, purchases are typically not quick decisions. The ability to work with a client over some time and gradually persuade them to invest in a piece takes time, skill, patience, and tact.

To Be a Successful Art Dealer, You Should . . .

- enjoy searching for and acquiring works of art
- be familiar with the Internet
- have patience to deal with artists and clients
- have strong business and sales skills
- be willing to continue to educate yourself about art and changes in the industry
- have excellent communication skills
- have a deep love of art

"In the art world," Howard says, "those of us who are not only successful, but have stood the test of time are confident in themselves, experts in their field, passionate about their work, and, above all, patient with their clients."

HOW DO I BECOME AN ART DEALER?

Education

High School

You can become an art dealer with a high school diploma, though many successful dealers have become specialists in their field partly through further education. While in high school, concentrate on history and art classes to familiarize yourself with the particular significance and details of different periods in time and the corresponding art of the period.

English and speech classes to improve communication skills are also helpful. Taking a foreign language (Howard recommends French) will also be useful. Art dealing is a people-oriented business. For this reason, it's crucial to be able to deal efficiently with different types of people and situations. Operating your own small business will also require skills such as accounting, simple bookkeeping, and marketing, so business classes are recommended.

Postsecondary Training

While a college education is not required, a degree in fine arts, art history, or history will give you a working knowledge of the pieces you sell and the historical periods from which they originated. Another option is obtaining a degree in business or entrepreneurship. Such knowledge will help you to run a successful business.

Howard worked part time under his father during his teenage years and went on to study art history at New York University. Around that time, his parents surprised him with some news. "My parents took me to London and informed me that I would be spending the next year living in Europe, buying all the works for the gallery. It was a 'learn-by-doing' experience." Howard also recommends that students develop an "eye" for art by working for art galleries during their summer breaks. "While book knowledge is great," he says, "what makes a dealer successful is their ability to see the good from the bad. The only way to do this is by seeing enough of both so you become an 'expert' in the period you want to deal in."

Certification and Licensing

Presently, there are no certification programs available for art dealers. However, if you plan to open your own gallery, you will need a local business license or permit.

In addition, if you wish to conduct appraisals, it will be necessary to take appraisal courses that are appropriate for your interest or art specialty. Certification is not required of those interested in working as an appraiser, but it is highly recommended, according to the International Society of Appraisers (ISA)—which administers an accreditation and certification program to its members. Obtaining accreditation or certification will demonstrate your knowledge and expertise in

A Changing Marketplace

Web sites and books that list the prices of works of art that have sold in public sales are changing the way the buying public interacts with art dealers.

"I think the most challenging aspect when we first meet a new client," says art dealer Howard Rehs, "are those people who enter the gallery feeling that they know more than we do about the prices of the works we offer. They may be unaware that the auction rooms are not the only place dealers buy their works, that an auction takes place at a very specific period in time, and there are many factors that enter into the price something brings at auction (quality, condition, period, size, weather on sale day, economic climate on that day, how well the sale was advertised, etc.)—most of which the book/Internet will not give you."

Howard says that buyers need to understand that not every painting offered at auction is a good example by the artist. And, that at times, fakes are sold at auction, which can create an inaccurate picture of the artist's desirability.

"While it is true that a decade or so ago most works came on the market through the auction rooms," Howard says, "the growth of the Internet has enabled many sellers to find those dealers who are leaders in their field and deal directly with them. This is not only a bonus for both the seller and dealer (because it cuts out the middleman—the auction room—who can take as much a 40 percent from the transaction), but for the gallery's ultimate client as well."

Before they purchase art, Howard believes that people first need to educate themselves about which galleries are considered industry leaders in their respective specialties. "[At the Rehs Galleries] we pride ourselves on not only the quality and condition of the paintings we offer," he says, "but the fact that the works will be outstanding examples of those artists' work. The art market is not always heading up, and when the downward trend begins, those individuals who have bought a great work in great condition will find that the value holds and will find ready buyers. Those individuals who purchased inferior quality work will have difficulty selling at almost any price."

appraisal and attract customers. To obtain accreditation, candidates must have three years of experience in appraising, complete the ISA Core Course in Appraisal Studies, and pass an examination. In order to become certified, individuals must complete additional training in their specialty area, submit two appraisals for peer review, complete professional development study, and pass a comprehensive examination.

Internships and Volunteerships

Opportunities to intern or volunteer exist in art galleries, museums, and art shops all over the country. Even simply visiting these sites regularly will give you knowledge and exposure to different works from various time periods. Another way to get experience in this field is by collecting pieces yourself. Art dealers' businesses often result from an overabundance of their personal collections. There are many ways to build your collection and create an inventory worthy of an art business. Attending yard sales is an inexpensive way to build your inventory; you'll never know what kind of valuables you will come across. Flea markets, local art galleries, and antique malls will also provide great purchasing opportunities and give you the chance to check out the competition.

WHO WILL HIRE ME?

Many art dealers are self-employed, operating their own galleries or renting space. Others operate solely through traveling art shows or through mail order or online catalogs. Some dealers prefer to work as employees of larger art galleries. In general, the more well known the dealer, the more permanent and steady the business. Prestigious auction houses such as Christie's or Sotheby's are attractive places to work, but competition for such jobs is fierce.

WHERE CAN I GO FROM HERE?

For those working out of their homes or renting showcase space at malls or larger shops, advancement in this field can mean opening your own art gallery. Besides a business license, dealers who open their own stores need to apply for a seller's permit and a state tax identification number.

At this point, advancement for art dealers is based on the success of their business. To ensure that their business thrives and expands, dealers need to develop advertising and marketing ideas to keep their business in the public's eye. Besides using the local library or Internet for ideas on opening their own businesses, newer dealers often turn to people who are already in the art business for valuable advice.

Howard Rehs would like to continue working in the field for as long as possible.

Related Jobs

- archivists
- art appraisers
- art conservators
- art critics
- art historians
- art teachers
- auctioneers
- buyers
- ceramic artists
- conservation technicians
- curators
- exhibit designers
- fine arts packers
- gallery directors
- historians
- merchandise displayers
- museum technicians
- multimedia artists
- painters
- retail managers
- retail sales workers
- sculptors

"A 90-year-old dealer," he says, "sounds good to me! I plan on continuing work on, and finishing, the catalogue raisonnés I began more than 10 years ago, and hope to continue working on additional scholarly projects. I am a firm believer in giving something back to the field that has given so much to me. I see the gallery as a leader in the area of 19th- and 20th-century art, and we are working hard at solidifying that position. I also feel it is important to find 'new' talent that meshes well with the type of 'old' art we currently deal in. Good contemporary artists need the support of the art world. I also hope that one, if not both, of my children decides to continue in the business—adding a fourth generation to our history."

WHAT ARE THE SALARY RANGES?

It is difficult to gauge what art dealers earn because of the vastness of the industry. Some internationally known, high-end art galleries dealing with many pieces of priceless works of art may make millions of dollars in yearly profits. This, however, is the exception. It is impossible to compare the high-end dealer with the lower end market. The majority of art dealers are comparatively small in size and type of inventory. Some dealers work only part time or rent showcase space from established shops.

According to a survey conducted by the Antiques and Collectibles Dealer Association (ACDA), the average showcase dealer earns about $1,000 a month in gross profits. From there, each dealer earns a net profit as determined by the piece or pieces sold, after overhead and other business costs. Note that annual earnings vary greatly for art and antique dealers due to factors such as size and specialization of the store, location, the market, and current trends and tastes of the public.

WHAT IS THE JOB OUTLOOK?

According to the Antiques and Collectibles Dealer Association, the collectibles industry should enjoy moderate growth in future years. The Internet has quickly become a popular way to buy and sell art and antiques. Though this medium has introduced collecting to many people worldwide, it has also had an adverse affect on the industry, namely for dealers and businesses that sell art in more traditional settings such as a gallery or at a trade show. However, the ACDA predicts that the popularity of Web sites devoted to selling collectibles will level off due to people wanting to see (in person) items they are interested in purchasing.

Though the number of authentic art and collectibles—items more than 100 years old—is limited, new items will be in vogue as collectibles. Also, people will be ready to sell old belongings to make room for new, modern purchases. It is unlikely that there will ever be a shortage of inventory worthy of an art gallery.

Howard Rehs sees good employment prospects for art dealers. "There will always be a need for knowledgeable and honest dealers in the art world," he says. "If you can become a true expert in your specific field, you will always be able to find employment."

Art Teachers

SUMMARY

Definition
Art teachers educate students of all ages about art techniques, art therapy, art criticism and history, art education, and art administration.

Alternative Job Titles
Art educators

Salary Range
$28,000 to $46,000 to $88,000+

Educational Requirements
Bachelor's degree (elementary and secondary teachers); master's degree (college professors)

Certification or Licensing
Required by all states (elementary and secondary teachers)
None available (college professors)

Employment Outlook
About as fast as the average (elementary and secondary teachers)
Much faster than the average (college professors)

High School Subjects
Art
Foreign language
History

Personal Interests
Art
Photography
Teaching

According to high school art teacher Susan Christensen, two of the most important qualities for art educators are flexibility and creativity.

"One time when the sculpture wire did not arrive in time for class," she recalls, "we soldered paperclips for gesture figures. Another time, when I was teaching color theory, I had the students stand up when I called out different color combinations. They enjoyed the participation and had to think about what they were wearing."

Susan has also learned to be flexible and creative when working with special needs students. "One student only had the use of one arm," she says, "so we were able to use a vice to assist him on projects. Another time a student was sensitive to different textures, and I changed his watercolor paper to smooth paper, and he was fine. For a student who was not verbally communicative, I had cards with pictures on them so the student could show me what he needed."

In short, expect the unexpected in this interesting, rewarding, and highly creative career.

WHAT DOES AN ART TEACHER DO?

Art teachers instruct students of all ages how to produce, appreciate, and understand the fine arts. Like teachers in other fields, they develop teaching outlines and lesson plans, give lectures, facilitate discussions and activities, keep class attendance records, assign homework, and evaluate student progress. *Elementary school art teachers* instruct younger students in the basics of art, such as colors and basic drawing, while *secondary school art teachers* and *college art professors* generally specialize in one area of art, such as studio art, photography, ceramics, or computer imaging.

Art teachers work in schools, community centers, colleges, and museums around the country. Their specific job responsibilities depend on the age level for which they teach.

In the first and second grades, art teachers cover the basic art skills: drawing, coloring, and identifying pictures and colors. With older students, teachers may introduce new materials and art procedures, such as sketching still life or working with papier mâché. To capture attention and teach new concepts, they use arts and crafts projects and other interactive activities. Although they are usually required to follow a curriculum designed by state or local administrators, teachers study new learning methods to incorporate into the classroom, such as using computers to create and manipulate artwork.

Secondary school art teachers teach students more advanced art concepts, such as ceramics and photography, in addition to basic studio art. Though secondary teachers are likely to be assigned to one specific grade level, they may be required to teach students in surrounding grades. For example, a secondary school art teacher may teach illustration to a class of ninth-graders one period and advanced photography to high school seniors the next.

In the classroom, secondary school art teachers rely on a variety of teaching methods. Because their students are more mature, they often integrate lectures about artists, procedures, and art history in with studio time. This lecture time also may include opportunities for student discussion about famous works and their own work. Secondary art teachers may also show films and videos, use computers and the Internet, bring in guest speakers, and organize field trips to enhance learning and keep students engaged in the subject.

College and university faculty members teach art at junior colleges or at four-year colleges and universities. Most art professors teach in a specific and highly specialized art form, such as sculpture or painting. They also teach classes in non-studio art, such as art therapy, art criticism and history, art education, and art administration.

In addition to teaching, most art faculty members continue to produce art, conduct research, and write publications. Art professors may show their work in galleries or publish their research findings in various scholarly journals. The more a professor shows or publishes work, the more likely the professor can advance to becoming permanent, tenured faculty.

All art teachers and professors devote a fair amount of time to preparation outside of the classroom. They prepare daily lesson plans and assignments, grade papers and tests, and keep a record of each student's progress. Other responsibilities include communicating with parents, advisors, or students through written reports and scheduled meetings, keeping their classroom orderly, and decorating desks and bulletin boards to keep the learning environment visually stimulating. They also continue to study alternative and traditional teaching methods to hone their skills.

Most art teachers are contracted to work 10 months out of the year, with a two-month vacation during the summer. During their summer break, many continue their education to renew or upgrade their teaching licenses and earn higher salaries. Teachers in schools that operate year-round work eight-week sessions with one-week breaks in between and a five-week vacation in the winter.

WHAT IS IT LIKE TO BE AN ART TEACHER?

Susan Christensen has been an art teacher for 12 years. "Art is a part of everything in life," she says. "You can relate art to so many areas, such as history, math,

> ### To Be a Successful Art Teacher, You Should . . .
>
> - love learning and teaching others
> - be patient and self-disciplined
> - have strong organizational skills
> - have artistic ability
> - be creative
> - have strong communication skills

and science. For the most part, students enjoy art, and the 'hands-on' experiences for students with learning disabilities are great. One learns about themselves and their world through art."

Susan teaches art at Pleasant Valley High School in Chico, California. She arrives at her school early each day to set up her classroom. "During class," she says, "I greet the students, introduce projects, provide materials, and help students individually (I never sit down)." Susan teaches five periods, and her classes include regular education students, special education students (resource, special day, and severely handicapped students), and English language learners. Aides occasionally assist her with the special needs students. "At the end of the day," she says, "I make sure my roll is complete, attend any meetings or conferences, and get the room ready for the following day's lesson. At night, I review lessons, correct papers or projects, and plan for upcoming units." In addition to working with students, Susan must keep track of equipment and materials used during class and order supplies in order to be prepared for the next class.

Art teachers work in generally pleasant conditions, although some older schools may have poor heating or electrical systems. The work can seem confining, requiring them to remain in the classroom throughout most of the day. Elementary school art teachers have to deal with busy children all day, which can be tiring and trying.

Elementary and high school hours are generally 8:00 A.M. to 3:00 P.M., but art teachers work more than 40 hours a week teaching, preparing for classes, grading papers, and directing extracurricular activities. Similarly, most college art professors work more than 40 hours each week. Although they may teach only two or three classes a semester, they spend many hours preparing for lectures, examining student work, and conducting research.

DO I HAVE WHAT IT TAKES TO BE AN ART TEACHER?

Many consider the desire to teach a calling. This calling is based on a love of learning. Teachers of young children and young adults must respect their students as individuals, with personalities, strengths, and weaknesses of their own. They must also be patient and self-disciplined to manage a large group independently. Because they work with students who are at very impressionable ages, they should serve as good role models. Elementary and secondary teachers should also be well organized, as teachers must keep track of the work and progress of a number of different students.

If you aim to teach art at the college level, you should enjoy research in addition to producing and teaching art. Not only will you spend many years studying in school, but your whole career will be based on communicating your thoughts, ideas, and artwork to the public. People skills are important because you'll be dealing directly with students, administrators, and other faculty members on a daily basis. You should feel comfortable in a role of authority and possess self-confidence.

HOW DO I BECOME AN ART TEACHER?
Education
High School

To prepare for a career in art education, follow your school's college preparatory program and take advanced courses in English, mathematics, science, history, and government—in addition to art. Composition, journalism, and communications classes are also important for developing your writing and speaking skills.

Susan advises high school students to get as much experience as possible. "Volunteer [recreation, tutoring programs, etc.] to work with students," she says. "Talk to teachers and work as a teacher's aide to find out more about what they do (which is a lot more than just teaching)."

Postsecondary Training

Your college training will depend on the level at which you plan to teach. All 50 states and the District of Columbia require public elementary education teachers to have a bachelor's degree in either education or in the subject they teach. Prospective teachers must also complete an approved training program, which combines subject and educational classes with work experience in the classroom, called student teaching. Susan feels that her experience as a student teacher was very valuable in preparing her to work as a teacher. "The biggest lesson in student teaching was to learn how little we knew about our student's lives," Susan says. "It opened my eyes to be aware of different situations. Student teaching also helped me to master organizational skills such as managing time, equipment, and student transitions."

If you want to teach at the high school level, you may choose to major in art while taking required education courses, or you may major in secondary education with a concentration in art. Similar to prospective elementary teachers, you will need to student teach in an actual classroom environment.

Prospective professors need at least one advanced degree in art. The master's degree is considered the minimum standard, and graduate work beyond the master's is usually desirable. If you hope to advance in academic rank above instructor, most institutions require az doctorate. Your graduate school program will be similar to a life of teaching—in addition to attending seminars, you'll research,

Related Jobs

- art historians
- ceramic artists
- child care workers
- docents
- guidance counselors
- multimedia artists
- painters
- school administrators
- sculptors
- teacher aides

prepare articles for publication, and teach some undergraduate courses.

Certification and Licensing

Elementary and secondary art teachers who work in public schools must be licensed under regulations established by the state in which they teach. If they move to another state, teachers have to comply with any other regulations in their new state to be able to teach there, though many states have reciprocity agreements, which means they accept out-of-state licensure, thereby making it easier for teachers to change locations.

To become licensed, prospective art teachers must be knowledgeable in several art subjects and complete an approved teaching program with the appropriate course credits in both education and art and a period of student teaching. Many states are moving towards a performance-based evaluation for licensing. In this case, after passing the teaching examination, prospective teachers are given provisional licenses. Only after proving themselves capable in the classroom are they eligible for a full license.

Internships and Volunteerships

Interning as a teacher is difficult to do without first finishing your school and licensure requirements. However, while you are in a teacher training program, you will have to student teach, which is very similar to an internship.

Volunteering to teach is much easier. You can volunteer to teach art in places as varied as community centers, summer camps, scout troops, daycare centers, or park districts. Any organization that offers tutoring or mentoring to young children could use help in the arts. Volunteer for a peer tutoring program. Even if you are not teaching art, the experience working with younger children will be useful.

If you would like to teach art at the college level, you will begin looking for teaching experiences while in graduate school. First, you will need to develop a curriculum vitae (a detailed, academic resume), work on your art expertise and showings, assist with research, attend conferences, and gain teaching experience and recommendations. Because of the competition for tenure-track positions, you may have to work for a few years in temporary teaching positions. Some professional associations maintain lists of teaching opportunities in their areas. They may also make lists of applicants available to college administrators looking to fill an available position.

WHO WILL HIRE ME?

Susan was already teaching another subject at a school when the art teacher transferred to another site. "The administration placed me in the art department," she says. "Previously, I had taught one period of art in my first teaching assignment, but I was willing to go 'anywhere' to get my first job."

Art teachers are needed at public and private institutions, museums, day care centers, juvenile detention centers, community centers, and schools of the arts. Although rural areas maintain schools, more teaching positions are available in urban or suburban areas. Art teachers are also finding opportunities in charter schools, which are smaller, deregulated schools that receive public funding.

Colleges around the country employ professors in various art disciplines. Employment opportunities in higher education vary based on talent, education, and exposure. Because art positions are scarce and hugely popular, individuals need their doctorate, a number of published works, and a record of good teaching.

Professional organizations are an excellent way to stay current with the job market and continue to learn about the field. Susan is a member of the California Art Education Association. "Professional organizations are invaluable," she says. "I recommend being a member of local (if there is one), state, and national organizations. They lobby legislatures for art, advocate for our programs, and provide professional journals and materials. They

Art Glossaries on the Web

Artlex Art Dictionary
http://www.artlex.com

Glossary of Art Conservation Terms
http://www.chicagoconservation.com

InfoPlease: Glossary of Art Movements
http://www.infoplease.com/ipea/
A0106225.html

Study Art
http://www.sanford-artedventures.com/
study/study.html

World Images: Navigating the World of Art
http://www.worldimages.com/art_
glossary.php

are also a great network for ideas, mentors, resources, and conferences."

WHERE CAN I GO FROM HERE?

As elementary and secondary art teachers acquire experience or additional education, they can expect higher wages and more responsibilities. Teachers with leadership skills and an interest in administrative work may advance to serve as principals or supervisors, though the number of these positions is limited and competition is fierce. Another move may be into higher education, teaching art classes at a college or university. For most of these positions, additional education is required. Other common career transitions are into the business world, such as moving to advertising, graphic design, or other related fields.

At the college level, the normal pattern of advancement is from art instructor to assistant professor, to associate professor, to full professor. All four academic ranks are concerned primarily with teaching and research. College faculty members who have an interest in and a talent for administration may be advanced to chair of the art department.

WHAT ARE THE SALARY RANGES?

According to the U.S. Department of Labor, the median annual salary for elementary school teachers was $44,040 in 2005. The lowest-paid 10 percent earned $29,360 or less; the highest-paid 10 percent earned $70,000 or more. The median annual salary for secondary school teachers was $46,060 in 2005. The lowest-paid 10 percent earned $30,530; the highest-paid 10 percent earned $73,330.

The American Federation of Teachers reports that the average salary for beginning teachers with a bachelor's degree was $31,704 in 2004. The estimated average salary of all public elementary and secondary school teachers was $46,597.

College professors' earnings vary depending on the size of the school, the type of school (public, private, women's only), and by the level of position the professor holds. The U.S. Department of Labor reports that the median annual salary for postsecondary art teachers was $51,240 in 2005. Ten percent of college art teachers earned $28,680 or less and 10 percent earned $88,380 or more.

Benefits for art teachers typically include health insurance, sick pay, 401 (k) plans, and reimbursement for continuing education. Full-time college faculty may also receive stipends for travel related to research, housing allowances, and tuition waivers for dependents.

WHAT IS THE JOB OUTLOOK?

According to the *Occupational Outlook Handbook* (*OOH*), employment opportunities for teachers (grades K–12) are expected to grow as fast as the average for all occupations through 2014. The need to replace retiring teachers will provide many opportunities nationwide. However, the demand for art teachers will be much lower, because schools hire a limited number of art faculty. Additionally, there is a surplus of talented, qualified art professionals wanting to get into teaching. Positions in inner-city schools or rural areas may be easier to find.

The *OOH* predicts much faster than average employment growth for college and university professors through 2014. College enrollment is projected to grow due to an increased number of 18- to 24-year-olds, an increased number of adults returning to college, and an increased number of foreign-born students. Retirement of current faculty members will also provide job openings. Again, however, full-time, tenure-track art positions are scarce and the competition for such positions is strong. Prospective art professors who are qualified, talented, and flexible (willing to move—even to another state) will have the most luck.

Art Therapists

SUMMARY

Definition
Art therapists treat and rehabilitate people with mental, physical, and emotional disabilities.

Alternative Job Titles
None

Salary Range
$25,000 to $60,000 to $80,000+

Educational Requirements
Master's degree

Certification or Licensing
Required by all states

Employment Outlook
About as fast as the average

High School Subjects
Art
Health
Psychology

Personal Interests
Art
Helping people: emotional health
Helping people: physical health/medicine

Nightmares tormented the three-year-old girl.

She had recently seen an image of a monster on her family's computer. Since then, her parents told art therapist Linda McCarley that their daughter hadn't been able to sleep in her own bed for weeks.

"The parents were frustrated because their daughter was now sleeping with them and nobody was getting a good night's sleep," Linda recalls.

"In her first session, I invited her to draw while telling me about the monster she had seen on the computer. She scribbled continuously as she described her fearful experience of seeing the monster. She discovered she could draw the monster in many different sizes and colors, and she

was able to tell stories about the monster and change the outcome." After Linda worked with the little girl for three sessions of drawing, painting, and talking, she was able to sleep peacefully through the night.

"The art therapy sessions enabled her to overcome her fear and regain a sense of control," Linda explains.

WHAT DOES AN ART THERAPIST DO?

Art therapists treat and rehabilitate people with mental, physical, and emotional disabilities. They use the creative processes of art in their therapy sessions to determine the underlying causes of problems and to help patients achieve therapeutic goals. Art therapists work with a wide range of art media, such as painting, sculpture, drawing, or photography. What they do with the art form depends on the specific needs of the patient and the setting of the therapy program.

Similar to dreaming, art therapy taps into the unconscious and gives people an uncensored mode of expression. This is important because before patients can begin to heal, they must first identify their feelings. Once they recognize their unconscious thoughts, they can begin to develop an understanding of the relationship between their thoughts and their feelings and behaviors.

The art therapist's main goal is to improve the client's physical, mental, and emotional health. After determining the strengths, limitations, and interests of their client, they create a treatment plan to promote positive change and growth. How these goals are reached depends on the unique specialty of the therapist as well as each client's desire to engage in creative growth and change.

Art therapists work with all age groups: young children, adolescents, adults, and senior citizens. They can work in individual, group, or family sessions. The approach of the therapist, however, depends on the specific needs of the client or group. For example, if a client is feeling overwhelmed by too many options or stimuli, the therapist may give him or her only a plain piece of paper and a pencil to work with that day.

To reach their patients, art therapists use art therapy interventions to improve a patient's self-confidence and self-awareness, to relieve states of depression, and to improve physical dexterity. The art therapist encourages and teaches patients to express their thoughts, feelings, and anxieties via sketching, drawing, painting, or sculpting. Art therapy is especially helpful in revealing patterns of domestic abuse in families. Children involved in such a situation may depict scenes of family life with violent details or portray a certain family member as especially frightening or threatening.

Art can also be used with the elderly. An art therapist treating a patient with Alzheimer's might ask the client to draw a childhood home from his or her past, thus stimulating long- and short-term memory, soothing feelings of agitation, and increasing a sense of reality.

WHAT IS IT LIKE TO BE AN ART THERAPIST?

Linda McCarley has been a registered art therapist since 1993. How did Linda become interested in art therapy? "I realized I had a strong interest in psychology as well as in art," she explains. "I began searching for ways to merge my interests and discovered the profession of art therapy. I decided to attend the annual conference of the American Art Therapy Association to learn more and to gain assurance that this was a profession I wished to pursue. Attending the conference helped me realize that this path would be a good fit for me."

Linda works in both private practice and is the director of the Art Therapy

Institute, an independent educational institute in Dallas, Texas, that offers training to mental health professionals who wish to specialize in art therapy and work toward the credential of registered art therapist. As an art therapist working with clients in private practice, Linda must first determine the client's presenting and underlying problems. "I ask the client to draw pictures or create a collage so we can visualize some of the problems and discover additional factors," she says. "Then, if the client is willing, we determine what changes are desired, and it helps to draw these ideas as well. We can list the goals of art therapy and decide how we will know when they have been achieved and what must be done to accomplish them." In addition to working with patients, Linda also supervises interns and other therapists.

As the director of the Art Therapy Institute, Linda is "responsible for all business and educational operations including admissions, curriculum design and implementation, records, finances, communications, public relations, faculty and supervisors, finances, budgeting, and teaching."

Most art therapists work a typical 40-hour, five-day workweek; at times, however, they may have to work extra hours. The number of patients under a therapist's care depends on the specific employment setting. Most buildings are pleasant, comfortable, and clean places in which to work, and some facilities provide a studio environment specifically for art therapy.

To Be a Successful Art Therapist, You Should . . .

- be able to work well with patients and coworkers
- have strong communication skills
- have a strong desire to help others
- have compassion for the ill
- possess patience to work with sometimes uncooperative or challenging patients
- have excellent business skills if you plan to own your own business

DO I HAVE WHAT IT TAKES TO BE AN ART THERAPIST?

To succeed in this line of work, you should have a strong desire to help others seek positive change in their lives. "You must have compassion to work with people who are experiencing a great deal of sadness, tragedy, delusions, or emotional pain," Linda says, "and the patience to work with people who, at times, may be uncooperative or resistant to receiving help." Art therapists must have the patience and the stamina to teach and practice therapy with patients who may be resistant to help and slow to trust. A therapist must always keep in mind that even a tiny amount of progress might be extremely significant for some patients and their families. A good sense of humor is also a valuable trait.

HOW DO I BECOME AN ART THERAPIST?

Education

High School

To become an art therapist, you will need a bachelor's degree, so take classes that will prepare you for college-level classes. You should become as proficient as possible with the methods and tools related to the type of art therapy you wish to pursue. When therapists work with patients, they must be able to concentrate on the patient while also supporting the use of art tools and techniques. For example, if you want to become involved in therapy through sculpture, you need to be familiar with all the details of the craft before applying it to help patients.

In addition to art courses, you should consider taking an introductory class in psychology. Communication classes will give you an understanding of the various ways people interact, both verbally and nonverbally.

Postsecondary Training

To become an art therapist, you must earn at least a bachelor's degree in studio art, art education, or psychology with a strong emphasis on art courses as well. You will need to take a minimum of 18 semester hour credits (or 27 quarter-hour credits) of study in studio art, and a minimum of 12 semester hour credits (or 18 quarter-hour credits) of study in psychology, which must include developmental psychology and abnormal psychology. You will also need a graduate degree before you can become credentialed as a professional or advance in your chosen field. Linda attended an institute to acquire her education in art therapy and also completed a master's degree in social work, which enables her to practice independently. "Completing a master's degree requires rigorous academic work and a strong commitment to complete the requirements," she says.

Requirements for admission to graduate schools and post-graduate certificate programs vary by program, so contact the programs you are interested in to find out about their admissions policies. You will also be required to submit a portfolio of your original artwork along with the written application. Professional organizations can be a good source of information regarding high-quality programs. For example, the American Art Therapy Association provides a list of schools that provide master's degrees that meet their standards at its Web site, http://www.art-therapy.org. You can also view a complete list of postgraduate certificate programs.

In graduate school or in a postgraduate certificate program, your study of psychology and art will be in-depth. Classes may include group art psychotherapy, foundation of creativity theory, art assessment and treatment planning, and art therapy presentation. In addition to classroom study, you will also complete an internship or supervised practicum (that is, work with clients). Depending on your program, you may also need to write a thesis or present a final artistic project before receiving your degree.

Certification and Licensing

The Art Therapy Credentials Board offers registration and certification to art health, or marriage and family therapy. In some states, art therapists need licensing depending on their place of work. For specific information on licensing in your field, you will need to check with your state's licensing board. Therapists are also often members of other professional associations, including the American Psychological Association, the American Association of Marriage and Family Therapists, and the American Counseling Association. Linda is a member of the American Art Therapy Association (AATA), the National Association of Social Work, and the American Play Therapy Association. "I recommend that new art therapists join the AATA as well as any other professional organization which relates to their training and licensure," she advises. "It is important to stay informed about trends and changes in the profession."

Internships and Volunteerships

While working toward certification, art therapists often work as interns or assistants under established therapists. Unpaid training internships often can lead to a first job in the field.

Therapists who are new to the field might also consider doing volunteer work at a nonprofit community organization, correctional facility, or local association to gain some practical experience.

WHO WILL HIRE ME?

Linda worked as a social work/art therapy intern at the Dallas Child Guidance Clinic (currently known as the Dallas Child and

therapists. Therapists may receive the Art Therapist Registered (ATR) designation after completing a graduate or postgraduate certificate program and having some experience working with clients. For further certification, therapists can earn the Art Therapist Registered-board Certified (ATR-BC) designation by passing an additional written exam. To retain certification status, therapists must complete a certain amount of continuing education.

Many registered art therapists also hold additional licenses in other fields, such as social work, education, mental

Family Guidance Centers). When she completed her internship, she was hired by the clinic as a therapist. "I provided clinical social work and art therapy for children and their families at this location for five years," she says.

Art therapists usually work as members of an interdisciplinary health care team that may include physicians, nurses, social workers, psychiatrists, and psychologists. Although often employed in hospitals, therapists also work in rehabilitation centers, nursing homes, day treatment facilities, shelters for battered women, pain and stress management clinics, substance abuse programs, hospices, and correctional facilities.

Experienced art therapists might choose to be self-employed, working with patients in their own private practice studios. In such a case, the therapist might work more irregular hours to accommodate patient schedules. Other therapists might maintain a combination of service contract work with one or more facilities in addition to a private caseload of clients referred to them by other health care professionals. Whether therapists work on service contracts with various facilities or maintain private practices, they must deal with all of the business and administrative details and worries that go along with being self-employed.

Many art therapists work with children in preschools, grammar schools, and high schools, either as general therapists or special teachers. Some art therapists teach or conduct research in the creative arts at colleges and universities. Others teach in postsecondary academic settings.

WHERE CAN I GO FROM HERE?

With more experience, therapists can move into supervisory, administrative, and teaching positions. Often, the supervision of interns can resemble a therapy session. The interns will discuss their feelings and ask questions they may have regarding their work with clients. How did they handle their clients? What were the reactions to what their clients said or did? What could they be doing to help more? The supervising therapist helps the interns become competent art therapists.

Many art therapists have represented the profession internationally by speaking

Related Jobs

- art teachers
- bibliotherapists
- ceramic artists
- dance/movement therapists
- drama therapists
- horticultural therapists
- Hypnotherapists
- multimedia artists
- music therapists
- painters
- poetry therapists
- psychiatrists
- psychologists
- recreational therapists
- sculptors
- social workers

about the field to the media and at seminars and workshops. Raising the public and professional awareness of art therapy is an important concern for many therapists.

WHAT ARE THE SALARY RANGES?

A therapist's annual salary depends on experience, level of training, and education. Working on a hospital staff or being self-employed also affects annual income. According to the American Art Therapy Association (AATA), entry-level art therapists earned annual salaries of approximately $25,000 in 2003. Median annual salaries ranged from $28,000 to $38,000, and the top earnings for salaried administrators ranged from $40,000 and $60,000 annually.

The AATA reports that art therapists who have Ph.D.s and are licensed for private practice can earn between $75 and $90 per hour. However, those in private practice must pay professional expenses such as insurance and office rental fees.

The annual salary for therapists working for the government is determined by the agency they work for, their level of education and experience, and their responsibilities.

Benefits depend on the employer but generally include paid vacation time, health insurance, and paid sick days. Those who are in private practice must provide their own benefits.

WHAT IS THE JOB OUTLOOK?

The AATA notes that this is a growing field. Demand for new therapists is cre-ated as medical professionals and the general public become aware of the benefits gained through art therapies. Despite this growth, Linda says that the employment outlook for art therapists will likely vary depending on locale. "Some areas of the country will have a much greater need than others," she says. "If there are an abundance of art therapists in the region, naturally, the job market will be more competitive. If recognition of art therapy has not yet been developed in an area, the art therapist may need to educate and advocate for the creation of a position."

Although enrollment in college therapy programs is increasing, new graduates are usually able to find jobs. In cases where an individual is unable to find a full-time position, a therapist might obtain service contracts for part-time work at several facilities.

Job openings in facilities such as nursing homes should continue to increase as the elderly population grows over the next few decades. Advances in medical technology and the growing practice of discharging patients early from hospitals should also create new opportunities in managed care facilities, chronic pain clinics, and cancer care facilities. The demand for therapists of all types should continue to grow as more people become aware of the need to help disabled patients in creative ways. "Employment will be best for those who are also licensed to practice independently as a mental health professional," Linda says. "Counselors, social workers, and marriage and family therapists who are both licensed and also credentialed as registered art therapists will likely be in most demand."

Ceramic Artists

SUMMARY

Definition
Ceramic artists work with clay to create both functional and purely aesthetic objects.

Alternative Job Titles
Ceramists
Clay artists
Potters

Salary Range
$20,000 to $41,000 to $100,000+

Educational Requirements
Some postsecondary training

Certification or Licensing
None available

Employment Outlook
About as fast as the average

High School Subjects
Art
History

Personal Interests
Art
Building things

One thing Ron Starr has learned in his 31 years as a ceramic artist is that accidents happen—often when you think you know it all. "I think the art has a feel for when the artist begins to think he/she knows it all," he says.

This adage was proven in a major way back in 2001 when Ron received his newest kiln. The extremely powerful kiln, which he still uses today, weighs 7,000 pounds, has an 80 cubic ft. interior, and churns out about 1M BTUs of heat.

"I couldn't wait for my first firing," Ron recalls. "I loaded new work and was very excited about the pieces I had created. I turned on what I thought was just the pilot light to allow the work to fire slowly. But I accidentally turned the burners on high and within one minute blasted two fire streams with 1M BTUs into the kiln. Needless to say, I had destroyed the entire kiln load of work."

The next day Ron found a small ceramic statue a little girl had made for him. "I placed it above my kiln door, and it was my new kiln god. From that day forward I haven't had any major problems in my firings. In short: respect the earth (clay), the fire, and the art of making art."

WHAT DOES A CERAMIC ARTIST DO?

Ceramic artists—also known as *potters, ceramists, sculptors,* and *clay artists*—work with clay to make both functional and purely aesthetic objects. They blend basic elements (such as clay and water) and more specialized components (such as texture fillers, colorants, and talc) and form the mixture into shapes. They then use glazing and firing techniques to finish their pieces. Depending on the artists' individual preferences, they use either manual techniques or wheel throwing techniques to create such things as functional pottery (like coffee cups and vases), beads, tiles, architectural installations, and sculptures.

The particular properties of clay influence artists' decisions about what they are going to make—be it functional or purely aesthetic—and how they are going to make it. For some ceramic artists, shape and form are all-important. For others, throwing on the wheel is what matters most. In any case, clay is the basis. Different types of clay—like ball clay, earthenware clay, and stoneware clay—are dug from deposits in a soft and pliable form. To become hard and permanent after shaping, each type of clay needs to be fired to a certain temperature in an open fire or a kiln. The variations in the size of the clay particles and the different temperatures at which clays reach their maturity (correct hardness) produce the differences in texture and appearance among different pieces. For instance, earthenware clay is fired at low temperatures and does not become as dense as clays like porcelain and stoneware, which are fired at higher temperatures.

Although each artist works the clay in a unique way, there are some basic methods that can be used to define the nature of an artist's work. Some ceramic artists build their objects almost completely by hand,

not using a potter's wheel; others use a wheel to mold their forms; others make molds and pour clay into them. Handbuilding allows a potter to build free-form art, while the potter's wheel aids in making symmetrically shaped works. In both cases, the artist must prepare the clay by *wedging,* which involves throwing the clay body down hard against a flat surface or simply kneading it. Wedging removes air bubbles and provides a consistent level of moisture throughout the clay.

In handbuilding, an artist uses either the coil or the slab method. The coil method entails forming long rods of clay, coiling the rods into a desired shape, and blending the coils to create a smooth surface. With slabs, the artist simply joins pieces of clay together to make a pot or other shape. Before actually joining the slabs or coiling, the artist must *score* the adjoining edges—that is, lightly nick them to create a rough surface—and add watery clay, which is known as slip. This process helps the clay pieces stick together.

When using a potter's wheel, ceramic artists place a wedged piece of clay in the middle of the wheel, center the clay body so that a symmetrical shape can be formed, and push down the center of the solid clay body to begin forming walls. Shaping a pot involves skilled hand movements that cause the clay to bend and constrict as desired.

Once a pot is taken off the wheel, it is left to dry until it is as hard as stiff leather. At that time, the artist places the clay body back on the wheel to trim off any uneven edges and form a base. The artist can paint the body or apply slip to add texture at this point. When the body is bone dry, it is placed into an open fire or a kiln for several hours. Afterward, the artist applies glaze and fires the body again.

Pouring clay into a mold and throwing it on a wheel is called *jiggering;* mass-produced objects like sinks and jars are often made this way. But many potters and sculptors create single objects by pressing or pouring clay into molds without using the wheel. They use hump molds (any material over which you can press clay), plaster press molds, polystyrene foam molds, or other creative types of molds (one artist used a shark's head; another used a motorcycle guard).

A *production potter* is a ceramic artist who makes household items, but often makes what is called studio pottery—vases, bowls, and other pieces made more for display than for everyday use. These potters might work alone in a studio or with one or two colleagues or helpers, or they might set up a large workshop employing several people.

Other artists concentrate on specific niches in which they enjoy producing objects considered both functional and artful. Bead making, tile making, and the making of architectural ceramics are a few examples of creative endeavors. *Architectural ceramists* work on such things as tile-decorated subway stations, ceramic-clad building columns, and other types of sculptural installations in public settings like museums, shopping malls, and parks.

The *ceramic sculptor* creates works of art rather than functional pottery. Using clay and often other types of art media,

To Be a Successful Ceramic Artist, You Should . . .

- have strong artistic ability
- not be afraid to get dirty—creating ceramic art can be messy, but fun
- be willing to work very hard to develop a reputation in the field
- be patient when creating complicated or time-consuming pieces
- have an excellent imagination and a willingness to try new techniques and styles
- have good marketing skills
- be willing to pursue continuing education to improve your skills and knowledge

sculptors handbuild more than they throw on the wheel.

WHAT IS IT LIKE TO BE A CERAMIC ARTIST?

The life of an artist can be hugely rewarding, fulfilling, and enlightening. For all ceramic artists, the creative process must be an elemental part of their existence. Whether they are a functional potter, a sculptor, or a tile maker, this creative process is the most significant condition of their work.

Ron Starr has been a ceramic artist for 31 years—the last five of these years as a full-time artist. "I begin my day at around 6:00 or 7:00 A.M. with creative development," the Lake Zurich, Illinois–based artist says. "Since my work is all spontaneous, meaning there are no drawings, sketches, or predeterminations of what I'm going to produce, I begin by visualizing in my mind the general forms that I will produce that day. That would be sculptural vessels, wall pieces, or platters, etc. Next, I begin creating either sections of a piece or the entire piece, moving through the development stages completely spontaneously using the natural characteristics of the clay to create designs and surface textures." [To view photos of Ron's art and a video of him creating a work, visit http://www.ronstarrinc.com.] "Throughout my day, music is always playing in the background, coffee's hot, and I try to stay away from the phone and other distractions. When things appear to be on a roll creatively, I stay as long as possible and ride that creative process. If things are not flowing well, I determine a good place to stop in order to begin the next day hoping for good creative karma."

Depending on the quantity of work he has created, Ron then sets up various schedules for kiln loading and firings. "These firings range from 30 hours to seven days depending on the type of work, thickness, and size," he says. "A piece typically takes 10 days, plus drying time of approximately four weeks."

After lunch, Ron focuses on marketing his work. He uses direct mail, phone calls, and Internet/e-mail follow-up to tell people about his art.

Ceramic artists typically work in a studio at a school, a potter's workshop, or their basement or garage. An artist's work area often reflects the activity done there, the personality of the artist, and the techniques used to create the ceramic pieces. An artist's studio space doesn't have to be elaborate, but certain things—like spaciousness, ventilation, and lighting—should be considered. Health and safety issues should be considered as well; a studio should have a filter vacuum cleaner, venting system, and fire extinguisher.

The life of a professional ceramic artist is like that of other artists—the work is personally rewarding but perhaps difficult, with earned money and recognition often out of proportion to the training, time, and effort involved. Perhaps the most difficult task for the potter wanting his or her own studio is to be practical. They must consider costs for such things as the clay, kiln, fuel, chemicals, and the rental of studio space and utilities.

DO I HAVE I WHAT IT TAKES TO BE A CERAMIC ARTIST?

If you really want to be a ceramic artist, you can't be squeamish about getting up to your elbows in wet clay! Work clothes get splotched, caked, and stiff, and your hands get covered in clay.

As with all art careers, you must have talent and patience to succeed as a ceramic artist. Artists must truly love what they do, because it can take time to develop a reputation and body of work worthy to sell in the open market.

As a ceramic artist, your imagination is always on call. While a standard cooking pot or coffee mug might be ordinary looking, ceramic art typically is not. To distinguish their creations from the ordinary and compete with other artists, the ceramic artist must stay imaginative and inspired, constantly evolving their work so that it stays fresh and appealing.

Ron Starr feels that successful ceramic artists should be disciplined, have good creative thinking skills, the ability to continually develop new work, the ability to market yourself and your work, and general business and administrative skills. He also recommends that ceramic artists

Related Jobs

- art conservators
- art dealers
- art historians
- art teachers
- conservation technicians
- curators
- gallery directors
- illustrators
- jewelers and jewelry repairers
- marble setters, tile setters, and terrazzo workers
- multimedia artists
- museum technicians
- painters
- photographers
- sculptors

pursue continuing education via books, audio tapes, workshops and classes, and networking.

HOW DO I BECOME A CERAMIC ARTIST?

Ron Starr began taking ceramic-related classes when he was a junior in high school and continued throughout his college years. "As soon as I started to work in clay back in high school," he says, "it became my favorite medium to work in." He graduated from the University of Wisconsin–Madison with a bachelor's degree in business administration and a minor in ceramic art.

Education

High School

While in high school, take pottery classes and other art classes, such as drawing and painting. It may also be helpful to take art history classes, so you can learn how architectural forms have evolved and how art styles are influenced.

Ruth Siporski has been a full-time ceramic artist since 1995. (You can view her work at http://www.brunnergallery. com.) She advises students to expose themselves to a wide variety of classes and activities to help them learn more about the field. "Take art if available," she advises, "but not just one media! If you are interested in ceramics also take drawing, design, sculpture . . . even chemistry. Look for freebee or cheap local workshops, art guilds, and local universities. Most art departments have visiting artists come in to demonstrate at little or no charge to students and guests."

Postsecondary Training

To further prepare yourself to become a ceramic artist, consider a postsecondary art program with a focus in ceramic art and design. You can choose from specialized art schools (the Art Institute of Chicago and the Maine College of Art, for example) or a number of general universities and colleges. It traditionally takes four years to get a bachelor of fine arts degree with a major in ceramic art. Courses include specifics like earthenware and stoneware. Design aspects of functional forms, such as plates, pitchers, and lidded containers, are explored in addition to learning how to get your pieces ready for the kiln and how to fire your work.

Visit the Web site (http://www.nceca.net) of the National Council on Education for the Ceramic Arts for a list of schools that offer degrees in ceramics.

Internships and Volunteerships

Although many artists follow a traditional educational path, there certainly are exceptions. Some ceramic artists are self-taught, having the discipline, motivation, and passion to learn on their own. Others get involved with apprenticeships or internships at potters' studios, learning from experienced artists who are willing to teach others who have strong dedication to the art. When first starting out, in particular, see if you can volunteer as an artist's assistant, helping with basic tasks such as cleaning the potter's tools, wheel, or other tasks. Museums also look for

interns or volunteers to help out; even as a tour guide you could learn a lot of useful information about famous ceramic art. Volunteering your time shows that you're interested in learning about a field.

Tips for Success

Ruth Siporski, a full-time ceramic artist, offers this humorous, yet relevant, set of rules that will help you to be successful in the field:

- Bend from the knees.

- If you are wondering if you are going to blow up your bisque kiln, you shouldn't have goofed off last week.

- If your pottery crates are smoking in the back of your van as you leave for your show, you shouldn't have goofed off last week.

- Wholesale versus retail . . . Do you want to make that thing over and over again for a whole year? Think about that before you bring that thing to market.

- If you have an idea, jump on it. There is someone else in the world having the same revelation.

- Evolve. The more successful you are, the more look-a-likes appear at the next show.

- Learn your production level and do not overestimate it. Stuff will always get in the way, so make time for the "stuff."

- Don't forget your dolly.

- Finally, play nice with the artist in the next booth. It may be a long show.

WHO WILL HIRE ME?

As for all other artists, it is difficult to earn a living by selling your pieces. Ceramic artists may have an advantage if they are able to produce functional objects as well as artistic pieces. Still, it's most likely that you will have to supplement your income by working another job.

Many artists go into teaching. Those who want to teach at a high school or university level should have a good background in other art forms because entry-level teaching positions often include teaching other art media, such as studio art, in addition to ceramics. You can also teach small workshops in your own studio, inviting people from different backgrounds and with different goals to learn ceramics. Ron Starr has taught at high schools, colleges, and in his community. Another avenue for teaching is in art therapy, which involves working with patients on a level that includes artistic creation as a way to help the healing process. For this job, you will need a background in psychology and health in addition to art.

Membership in professional organizations is also a good way to get your name out there and develop professionally. Ron is a member of the Potters Council, American Craft Society, and the American Ceramic Society. "I recommend membership in these organizations and any organization that offers networking and participation opportunities that help build your name and promote future sales," he says.

Ruth Siporski also recommends membership in professional associations. "The American Craft Council and National Council on Education for the Ceramic Arts are great organizations that provide a wonderful service to artists with education, information, opportunity, and support."

WHERE CAN I GO FROM HERE?

Ceramic artists who want to work on their own will have to consider renting studio space and showing their work somehow. Perhaps a gallery owner will want to include their pieces in his or her shop; maybe the school they attended will have a show and put their pieces on display there; or maybe someone will come into their studio one day and fall in love with what they're making. These are just a few possibilities for having work shown, appreciated, and bought.

Many artists feel that their goals lie in simply being able to work at their art, in whatever environment. They might not be especially concerned about whether their pieces sell to the public; they might be more satisfied to know that a limited group of people enjoy their work. Others want specifically to have their own studios, produce many pieces, and become famous in the art world. It depends on their desires, their own personality, and their concern with what brings fulfillment in their life's work.

WHAT ARE THE SALARY RANGES?

To most artists, earnings come in different forms, not just monetary wealth. Of course many would like to be success-

How to Create Ceramic Art

It takes a lot of work to create ceramic art. Here, in her own words, are the steps that Ruth Siporski takes when creating a work:

- Planning. I sketch all the time—patterns, shapes, and anything that catches my eye or pops out of my brain. Putting it on paper helps me remember those thoughts so I can convert them into vessels and sculptural components when I am planning the series of work to be constructed. I build in a very organized fashion . . . planning is necessary.

- Choose the series (usually six to eight of the same thing) and roll enough clay to build that group.

- Construct the forms, progressing through the series and making adjustments to a design as you go—hopefully getting better as you go.

- Carve, stamp, emboss, and detail the pieces. This gives the pieces texture and depth.

- Apply first phases of dark color, sand (leaving the dark color in the crevasses), and then allow to dry.

- Bisque the work.

- Glaze/fire—sometimes glazing and firing more than once to achieve a successful result.

- Use quality control. Remove seconds from the group. Make the galleries happy with rubber feet for protection, and you are finished.

doesn't happen with every ceramic artist. A ceramic artist might work hundreds of hours on one piece of sculpture, and finally realize that they don't want to part with it at all. They might be tremendously inspired, quickly throw an unusually good pot on the wheel, and immediately offer it for sale.

The U.S. Department of Labor reports that the median annual earning for fine artists (which includes painters, sculptors, and illustrators) was $41,280 in 2005. However, many ceramic artists make considerably less. Many artists who want to earn steady pay would be wise to work for an established potter or a large ceramics manufacturer. This type of job might pay $20,000 to $30,000 per year.

For many, being an artist is more satisfying than having a good income. Setting up one's own studio, being able to get involved in the creative process whenever inspiration strikes, working with clay—this is the type of living that many artists strive for. Ceramic artists who are self-employed will have to provide their own health insurance, paid vacations, and other fringe benefits. An extremely talented artist might earn more than $100,000 per year. However, it is also possible that this artist's pieces will lose popularity, and he or she will make only $20,000 the next year.

WHAT IS THE JOB OUTLOOK?

The *Occupational Outlook Handbook* predicts that the employment of artists and related workers is expected to grow about as fast as the average through

ful in terms of how many pieces they sell and how much money they make, but this

2014. However, it is very hard to predict whether ceramic artists will enjoy success and recognition in the near future. Within the broader art world—which includes painting, architecture, and sculpture—ceramic art and design is quite new. Ceramics instruction is widespread today, but as late as the 1930s, ceramics wasn't really considered much of an art. People today still debate whether it is a craft or an art.

However, there are good signs that ceramics as an art form has the potential to become well recognized. The last decade has produced many books, videos, and magazines on the subject, along with workshops, conferences, and competitions throughout the world. Ceramic artists gather to show their work, work together, and teach others. Many have made names for themselves in the art world and are valued as artists.

Gallery Directors

SUMMARY

Definition
Gallery directors are responsible for the profitable management and operation of art galleries.

Alternative Job Titles
Curators

Salary Range
$20,000 to $32,000 to $57,000+

Educational Requirements
High school diploma
Some postsecondary training recommended

Certification or Licensing
None

Employment Outlook
More slowly than the average

High School Subjects
Art
Business
Foreign language
Mathematics

Personal Interests
Art
Business
Photography
Selling/making a deal

Stephanie Walker says that two of her biggest priorities as a gallery director are keeping her clients and her artists happy. "Without either one of those," she says, "you simply don't have a gallery. And of course, working with both clients and artists presents a whole set of unique challenges."

One summer, Stephanie and her colleague were installing a group exhibit at her gallery. "There were six different artists who all had their own distinct style," she recalls. "We had to curate the exhibit so that all of the artists got equal representation and make sure that the paintings and sculptures all worked well together. That's a pretty standard challenge in the gallery business."

However, the task proved to be a little more difficult than usual. Stephanie and her colleague spent the entire day arranging and rearranging the work until they finally found the combination that worked best.

Everything seemed on track. They held a reception for the artists and everyone seemed pleased with the presentation—that is, until the next morning when Stephanie arrived at the gallery to find a voicemail that had been left in the middle of the night. "One of the artists absolutely hated the way we had installed the show," she says. "It was quite a shock because we have always been complimented on our installations, and everyone had seemed so pleased with this one." Stephanie called the artist to try to get a better sense of what his hopes had been. "I tried to explain that this was a group show and that we had worked hard to give everyone equal representation but, in all fairness, he truly had received the best placement. I explained that we had spent all day trying different combinations of paintings and that we felt pretty strongly that this was *the* combination. He persisted. I listened. I told him that I couldn't promise anything, but that I would give it a try.

"My colleague was really upset with the critique and terribly disappointed in me that I had 'caved in' to the will of an artist. I said that we owed it to him to at least try."

Stephanie and her colleague worked nearly six hours to rearrange the exhibit and finally saw what it was the artist had hoped for and installed an entirely new exhibit.

"In the end," Stephanie says, "the artist was thrilled and my colleague and I had become better curators as a result. These are the challenges that a gallery director lives for."

WHAT DOES A GALLERY DIRECTOR DO?

Gallery directors are responsible for every phase of a gallery's operation. They often are one of the first employees to arrive in the morning and the last to leave at night. The duties of gallery directors vary according to the type of art sold, the size of the gallery, and the number of employees. Their duties include working with artists and the public; researching and organizing exhibitions; writing catalogue or brochure copy for exhibitions; setting up exhibitions; hiring, training, and supervising employees; maintaining the physical surroundings of the gallery; hosting gallery tours; selling artwork; monitoring expenditures and receipts; fund-raising (if they are employed by a nonprofit gallery); corresponding with clients and artists; and marketing the gallery and its artists to the public (including writing press releases, being interviewed by the media, and updating the gallery's Web site). In small galleries, directors may handle all of these tasks. In large galleries that employ more staff, however, directors may be involved in only a few of these activities.

Most art galleries are pleasant, intellectually engaging places to work, and directors often have comfortable offices. Most art galleries are open five or more days a week. They are typically open during regular business hours, but many offer extended hours in the evening. Directors often work as many as 50 to 60 hours a week.

Directors should be good at working with all different kinds of people. Differences of opinion and personality clashes among employees are inevitable. Therefore, the manager must be able to restore good feelings among the staff. Directors may have to deal with difficult or upset customers and must attempt to restore goodwill toward the gallery when customers are dissatisfied.

Some gallery directors may travel to visit artists' studios, attend auctions, or participate in museum/art history conferences.

WHAT IS IT LIKE TO BE A GALLERY OWNER AND OPERATOR?

Stephanie Walker is the director of the Chase Gallery in Boston, Massachusetts. (You can learn more about the gallery by visiting http://www.chasegallery.com.) She has been the gallery's director for two years. "One of the most wonderful aspects of my job as director of a contemporary art gallery is that I get to work with living artists every day," she says. "I have to work very closely with these people, so oftentimes we establish great friendships and I become very involved in their personal lives. I have to say, it is very rewarding to know that you are helping a living artist make a career out of something they love and something that puts beauty into the world."

Stephanie says that one of the most exciting aspects of managing a gallery is that there is no "typical" day. "You have a sense of some of the things that you will be doing that day," she says, "but most of the time, the day unfolds on its own agenda. As the director, I am responsible for overseeing all of the daily operations of the gallery. My primary responsibilities include sales, managing the exhibition schedule, finding new artists, and overseeing my sales staff. Regular daily routines include discussing the current show that I have on exhibit, pulling paintings out of the back room for clients to view, writing personal letters, putting together packages, and making phone calls to clients. I am responsible for doing the portfolio review of potential new artists. I plan the exhibition schedule. I oversee the entire exhibition production, from writing press releases and gathering all relevant information for upcoming shows to getting the Web site ready, getting the work in the gallery, and getting it installed. Our gallery is a small business, so my responsibilities may also include everything from taking the garbage out, sweeping and cleaning the bathroom, to greeting people that come into the gallery."

Other gallery directors work at nonprofit galleries that are sponsored by academic institutions or foundations. Galleries that are sponsored by academic institutions are typically linked with the schools' art departments and offer educational and cultural opportunities to the surrounding community. They receive funding from their sponsor institution by applying for grants, by holding annual fund-raisers, and through other methods.

Julie Charmelo is the Director of the Northern Illinois University (NIU) Art Gallery in Chicago, Illinois. (To learn more about the gallery, visit http://www. vpa.niu.edu/museum/html/chicagogllry. html.) She has been its director since 1997. "Some of the best aspects of my job," she says, "include the freedom to explore artwork and artistic themes that interest you, the chance to interact with artists and visit their studios, the opportunity to express yourself through curatorial projects and publications, and being surrounded by art on a daily basis. My primary job duties consist of curating one to two group exhibitions of Chicago-area artists per year, writing and publishing a catalogue or brochure to accompany each show, organizing the NIU Art Museum's annual fund-raiser, visiting local artist studios, presenting gallery tours for visiting student and art-affiliate groups, and managing the gallery on a daily basis (including interacting with visitors, answering phones, responding to correspondence, reviewing artist slides, among other tasks)."

Julie shares her secondary duties with the staff of the NIU DeKalb galleries. "These include," she explains, "photographing exhibits, designing and printing exhibition announcement cards, applying for grants annually, cleaning and maintaining the gallery space, hanging and striking exhibits (four to five per year), and repairing the gallery space in between shows."

Julie says that she spends approximately 40 percent of each day on administrative duties, 30 percent on curatorial duties, 15 percent on fund-raising, 10 percent on studio visits, and 5 percent on gallery tours.

To Be a Successful Gallery Director, You Should . . .

- have good communication skills
- enjoy working with and supervising people
- be able to motivate your employees
- have strong problem-solving abilities
- have the ability to be diplomatic when dealing with artists and clients
- have strong business and sales skills
- possess physical strength in order to occasionally complete menial and/or physically demanding tasks

DO I HAVE I WHAT IT TAKES TO BE A GALLERY OWNER AND OPERATOR?

Whatever the experience and training, a gallery director needs a lot of energy, patience, and fortitude to overcome the slow times and other difficulties involved in running a business. Other important personal characteristics include maturity, creativity, and good business judgment.

Gallery directors should also have good communication skills and enjoy working with and supervising people. They also should be able to motivate employees and delegate authority. "When you work in a gallery, you deal with all kinds of personalities on a daily basis," Stephanie Walker says. "It can be a challenge at times. It's important to have strong interpersonal skills and even stronger communication and problem-solving skills."

Diplomacy often is necessary when dealing with artists. "The most difficult part of my job, though, is telling an artist no," Stephanie says. "We get hundreds of submissions every year from artists who are pouring their hearts and souls into their work. We have to say no to most of them. We can only take on one or two new artists per year. However, that does not mean that the work isn't good. Oftentimes, the work simply does not fit with our gallery."

Julie Charmelo believes that successful gallery directors need to have "strong organizational, research, and writing skills; an open, creative mind; the ability to perform physical labor (required for installations); and the patience to deal with artists and the public and to perform often menial, repetitive tasks."

HOW DO I BECOME A GALLERY OWNER AND OPERATOR?

Education

High School

You will need at least a high school diploma in order to become a gallery director. Helpful courses include art, history, business, mathematics, marketing, and economics. English and speech classes are also important. These courses will teach you to communicate effectively with all types of people, including artists, employees, and customers. Studying a foreign language may also be helpful.

High school activities that may give you useful experience include forming and managing an art club. "Volunteering as a docent at a local art museum is useful," Julie Charmelo recommends, "as is applying for an internship at local commercial and/or nonprofit galleries."

If you are creative in nature, try experimenting with different artistic styles and techniques. "I am an artist as well," Julie says, "although I'm not very devoted to my artistic career. I enjoy drawing, painting, and collage work, but photography is my preferred medium. I have spent a good deal of time lately doing portrait photography, especially of my infant daughter."

Postsecondary Training

You do not need a college degree to work as a gallery director, but a degree or at least some postsecondary education will certainly give you an advantage over other applicants in this highly competitive field. Many directors have degrees in art, art history, marketing, history, or business management. College courses that will help you to prepare for a career as a gallery director include art theory, art administration, art history, accounting, business, marketing, English, advertising, and computer science. All directors, regardless of their education, must have good marketing, analytical, communication, and people skills.

In addition to postsecondary training, Stephanie Walker stresses that it is critical for gallery directors to stay up-to-date with current trends in the industry. "I read *ARTnews, Art in America, ART + Auction,* and *ARTFORUM* every month," she says. "I travel to New York once a month. I try to get to as many of the major art fairs and gallery and museum shows as I can every year."

Internships and Volunteerships

Many postsecondary art programs require students to participate in at least one internship during their college careers—typically at an art gallery, a museum, an art manufacturer, or a related employer. Internships generally last between one and two semesters. Interns generally receive no pay, but their experience counts toward a predetermined number of credit hours.

Related Jobs

- appraisers
- archivists
- art appraisers
- art conservators
- art critics
- art dealers
- art teachers
- art historians
- auctioneers
- buyers
- ceramic artists
- conservation technicians
- curators
- exhibit designers
- fine arts packers
- merchandise displayers
- multimedia artists
- museum directors
- museum technicians
- painters
- photographers
- retail managers
- retail sales workers
- sculptors

WHO WILL HIRE ME?

Few people start their careers as gallery directors. Many start as *gallery assistants, art consultants,* or *assistant directors* or in some other position in the art industry.

Stephanie Walker says that she had no idea that she would pursue a career in the arts. In college, she earned a degree in sociology and took several art history classes. "After I graduated from college," she says, "I interviewed for all kinds of positions that would use my sociology degree, but never seemed to be able to find the perfect fit. One day, my boyfriend (now my husband) pointed out a help wanted ad in the local newspaper. The position was in a 19th century fine art gallery. I thought he was nuts. I didn't have a degree or any experience but he encouraged me to apply anyway. I did, and I got the job. It was a wonderful experience, and I knew at that point that gallery work was something I wanted to do." After moving to Boston and pursuing positions in the technology industry, Stephanie found a position with Chase Gallery as assistant director. After another hiatus from gallery work, she returned to Chase Gallery as a part-time art consultant and eventually took over the directorship. "I don't think that there is only one obvious way to get involved with a gallery," she says. "I certainly wouldn't trade my nongallery-related experiences for anything. They have made me better at what I do as the director."

Julie Charmelo followed a much more traditional path to become a gallery director. She earned both undergraduate and graduate degrees in art history. During her second year of graduate school, she applied for and was awarded a Lecturing Fellowship at the Art Institute of Chicago. "I participated in the program for one year," she says, "and have since continued on as an adjunct lecturer for the last nine years. I also worked as a curatorial intern at the Museum of Contemporary Art [Chicago] while in graduate school. After graduate school, I worked for a commercial gallery for one year before starting as director at the NIU Art Gallery in 1997."

WHERE CAN I GO FROM HERE?

Advancement opportunities for gallery directors vary according to the size, reputation, and location of the gallery and the interests of the director. Advancement also depends on the individual's work experience and educational background. Some directors may decide to open their own galleries after they have acquired enough experience. Others may work as writers, art consultants, and educators.

WHAT ARE THE SALARY RANGES?

Salaries for gallery directors depend on the size and reputation of the gallery and the director's job responsibilities. A director employed by a well-known gallery in New York, Chicago, or Boston typically earns more than a director employed at a gallery in a small town or rural area. Directors at commercial galleries usually earn higher salaries than those directors who are employed by nonprofit galleries. The U.S. Department of Labor cat-

Tips for Success

Stephanie Walker offers the following advice to aspiring gallery directors, in her own words:

- Love what you do. There is no better feeling than to be inspired in the morning to get out of bed to go to work because you love what you do.

- Do your research. There are all kinds of different galleries out there with different business models that represent different kinds of work. Galleries are small business so, although we all do the same basic things, we get there in very different ways.

- Be certain that a gallery is where you want to be before you apply. I often have people come into the gallery looking for a job in "the arts." Galleries are for-profit businesses. They are very different than museums or nonprofit cultural institutions.

- Educate yourself. This is true for any business, but in the arts, especially in the contemporary arts, there are so many different and new things happening all the time. Read trade magazines and visit galleries and museums.

- Don't give up. Galleries are run by a very small staff. Positions are coveted and do not open up often. Be prepared to do whatever it takes to get into a gallery. It is not unusual to have to take a part-time position for several years in a gallery before a full-time position opens up. If you are not fully committed to being in a gallery, it won't happen.

egorizes the career of gallery director under the more general heading of "retail manager." In 2005, these professionals had median annual earnings of $32,840. Salaries ranged from less than $20,500 to $57,420 or more annually.

Gallery directors typically receive full benefits, including health insurance, paid vacation, and sick leave.

WHAT IS THE JOB OUTLOOK?

The career of gallery director is a much-sought-after position in the art world. Applicants with strong educational backgrounds and work experience will have the best chances of finding jobs. Julie Charmelo sees fairly hopeful employment prospects for gallery directors. "Although the field is very competitive," she says, "there are still many opportunities available to those willing to work hard. In Chicago, in particular, there are numerous opportunities for young curators and artists, and a public who is open to emerging professionals." Overall, employment of retail managers in all industries is expected to grow more slowly than the average for all occupations through 2014, according to the U.S. Department of Labor.

Illustrators

SUMMARY

Definition
Illustrators create artwork for both commercial and fine art purposes.

Alternative Job Titles
None

Salary Range
$19,000 to $41,000 to $79,000+

Educational Requirements
High school diploma

Certification or Licensing
Voluntary

Employment Outlook
About as fast as the average

High School Subjects
Art
Computer science

Personal Interests
Art
Computers
Drawing

One of the first major lessons Will Terry learned as a new illustrator was to always get the fax—or, in other words, get any and all information from a potential employer so that you can get the assignment done.

The lesson began when Will received a call from an art director who was anxious to assign a project so she could attend a wedding over the upcoming weekend. "I was eager to accept the assignment because I was a beginning illustrator and I desperately needed the money," Will explains. "We discussed the assignment and agreed on a sketch date, due date, and fee. She was in a hurry to leave the office, so she said she'd put all of her contact information on the fax. I thought that would be a great idea because writing all of that info down would take 30 seconds and, shoot, faxes are fool proof."

Will hung up the phone and waited for her fax . . . which never came. "I guess I was too busy being excited about getting the job because I couldn't remember her name or where she worked or even what city she was in! You can't use directory assistance if you can't tell the operator anything about the person you wish to contact."

Will waited and waited for the art director to call, but the sketch date came and went with no call. The art director finally called five days after the sketch date deadline. "When we finally talked she wasn't very understanding. I think she thought

I should have at least remembered the company she worked for. There was only three days left before the final illustration was due and she had to give me a few extra days to finish the job—which also ticked her off."

Professional lesson learned: as an illustrator, don't rely on technology and always get a name and contact information whenever you work with clients.

WHAT DOES AN ILLUSTRATOR DO?

Illustrations are used to decorate, describe, inform, clarify, instruct, amuse, and draw attention. They appear in print and electronic formats, including books, magazines, newspapers, signs and billboards, packaging (for everything from milk cartons to CDs), Web sites, computer programs, greeting cards, calendars, stationery, and direct mail. Illustrators use a variety of media—pencil, pen and ink, pastels, paints (oil, acrylic, and watercolor), airbrush, collage, and computer technology.

Illustrators often work as part of a creative team, which can include graphic designers, photographers, and individuals, called *calligraphers,* who draw lettering. Self-employed illustrators work out of their homes or private offices. Illustrators work in almost every industry. Medical illustration and fashion illustration are two of the fastest-growing specialties. The following paragraphs discuss these and other specialties.

Medical illustrators use graphics, drawings, and photographs to make medical concepts and descriptions easier to understand. Medical illustrators provide illustrations of anatomical and biological structures and processes, as well as surgical and medical techniques and procedures. Their work is found in medical textbooks, magazines and journals, advertisements for medical supplies and pharmaceuticals, instructional films and videotapes, television programs, exhibits, lectures and presentations, and computer-assisted learning programs. Some medical illustrators create three-dimensional physical models, such as anatomical teaching models, models used for teaching medical procedures, and prosthetics. A medical illustrator may work in a wide range of medical and biological areas or specialize in a particular area, such as cell structure, blood, disease, or the eye. Much of their work is done with computers; however, they must still have strong skills in traditional drawing and drafting techniques.

Fashion illustrators work in a glamorized, intense environment. Their artistic focus is specifically on styles of clothing and personal image. Illustrators can work in a few different categories of the fashion field. They provide artwork to accompany editorial pieces in magazines such as *Glamour*, *Redbook*, and *Vogue* and newspapers such as *Women's Wear Daily.* Catalog companies employ fashion illustrators to provide the artwork that sells their merchandise. Fashion illustrators also work with fashion designers, editors, and models. They make sketches from designers' notes or they may sketch live models during runway shows or other fashion presentations. They may use pencils, pen and ink, charcoal, paint, or a combination of media. Fashion illustrators may work as freelancers, handling all the business aspects that go along with being self-employed.

Natural science illustrators create illustrations of plants and wildlife for print and Web, such as exhibit brochures at museums like the Smithsonian.

Cartoonists are illustrators who create work, often amusing in nature, that usually tells a story or relays a message. Most people think of comic strips as the only work of cartoonists. However they also illustrate for magazine articles, Web pages, product packaging, or other sources of visual art. The work of cartoonists can be serious and powerful in nature. For example, popular cartoonist Art Spiegelman has created graphic novels dealing with subjects as serious as concentration camps (*Maus: A Survivor's Tale*) to terrorist attacks (*In the Shadow of No Towers*).

Illustrators generally work in clean, well-lit offices. They spend a great deal of time at their desks, whether in front of a computer or at the drafting table. Medical illustrators are sometimes required to visit operating rooms and other health care settings. Fashion illustrators may be required to attend fashion shows and other industry events.

Many illustrators, such as fashion illustrators and cartoonists, create work on a regular publishing schedule, either for a monthly magazine or a daily comic strip. Working under deadline pressure can create a stressful and fast-paced work environment, but these illustrators typically thrive under the pressure and enjoy the competitive and demanding nature of the work.

WHAT IS IT LIKE TO BE AN ILLUSTRATOR?

Will Terry has been a full-time illustrator since 1992. His work has appeared in publications such as *Time, Money, Seventeen,* and *Better Homes and Gardens* and in national advertisements for Sprint, Pizza Hut, and FedEx, among others. He has also created illustrations for books published by Scholastic, Random House, Hooked on Phonics, and other companies. (To see examples of Will's work, visit http://www.willterry.com.)

Will begins his day by reading and answering e-mail and checking for and returning phone messages. "I rarely have a gap between assignments, so there are always things to cross off on my to-do list," he says. "If I have a new assignment I spend the day sketching, scanning, and manipulating my sketches in Photoshop. If I'm in the middle of a project I spend the day painting while watching TV or a DVD. When I'm painting, I can also phone a friend and chat while I work. I usually try to plan my hours so that I can finish my work around 5:00 P.M. so I can spend time with my family in the evening. When I'm on a hot assignment I often have to toss that schedule and work late into the night; sometimes I don't go to bed until after midnight."

Will has worked for magazines, newspapers, publishers, and advertising companies, as well as for packaging and point of purchase projects. "I regularly complete assignments for editorial clients as well as children's publishers," he says, "and I am trying to get more children's picture books. One of my more eclectic assignments was an illustration of a king for a large peel and stick toilet seat cover—'the thrown'."

Will also teaches illustration. He taught illustration classes at Brigham Young University for several years and is currently teaching his first class at the high school level. "I find that I am surprised at both the level of commitment from some of the students and disappointed in the lack thereof from others," he says. "I see this as my biggest challenge—teaching those who are hungry and managing those who could care less. I find that teaching forces me to be honest in my work in that I have to follow the same rules and principles that I teach. I'm excited when I see some of my students catching the 'creative bug' and working hard on their own."

DO I HAVE WHAT IT TAKES TO BE AN ILLUSTRATOR?

Illustrators must be creative, and, of course, demonstrate artistic talent and skill. They also need to be flexible. Because their art is often commercial in nature, illustrators must be willing to accommodate their employers' desires if they are to build a broad clientele and earn a decent living. They must be able to take suggestions and rejections gracefully.

Will believes that professionalism is one of the key skills to becoming a successful illustrator. "Sometimes I think it's the guys

To Be a Successful Illustrator, You Should . . .

- have artistic talent and skill
- be flexible regarding deadlines and assignments
- be able to take suggestions and rejections gracefully—especially if you work as a commercial illustrator
- have a strong curiosity and creativity
- have excellent business skills
- be able to manage a variety of tasks and assignments simultaneously
- have strong communication skills

who turn stuff in late, or deviate from their sketches, or have attitude that keep me in business," he says. "It's sad really. I try to joke with some of my students about these issues, but I'm actually amazed at how many times I hear about illustrators with poor work habits. In the end I suppose it's Darwinian—the only illustrators that maintain a business are the ones who understand professionalism."

HOW DO I BECOME AN ILLUSTRATOR?
Education
High School

Creative talent is more important in this field than education. However, there are academic programs in illustration at most colleges and universities. If you are considering going on to a formal program, be sure to take plenty of art classes while in high school. Elective classes in illustration, ceramics, painting, or photography are common courses offered at many high schools.

Will recommends that students who are really interested in art should just start drawing. "Don't wait for an invitation," he advises. "Find art that you like, collect samples of it, read about the artists, give yourself an assignment, make your own art, show your art to other artists, and thank them for some honest criticism. If you have art classes in high school, take them, but be careful about gauging your performance against your peers because most of them will not care about the class as much as you do."

Postsecondary Training

To find a salaried position as a general illustrator, you should have at least a high school diploma and preferably an associate's or bachelor's degree in commercial art or fine art. Whether you are looking for full-time employment or freelance assignments, you will need an organized collection of samples of your best work, which is called a portfolio. Employers are especially interested in work that has been published or printed. An advantage to pursuing education beyond high school is that it gives you an opportunity to build your portfolio.

Medical illustrators are required to earn a bachelor's degree in either biology or art and then complete an advanced degree program in medical illustration. These programs usually include training in traditional illustration and design techniques, computer illustration, two-dimensional and three-dimensional animation, prosthetics, medical computer graphics, instructional design and technology, photography, motion media production, and pharmaceutical advertising. Course work will also include pharmacology, basic sciences including anatomy and physiology, pathology, histology, embryology, neuroanatomy, and surgical observation and/or participation.

Fashion illustrators should study clothing construction, fashion design, and cosmetology in addition to taking art courses. They should also keep up with the latest fashion and illustration trends by reading fashion magazines.

Related Jobs

- art dealers
- art directors
- art teachers
- ceramic artists
- gallery directors
- graphic designers
- multimedia artists
- painters
- police artists
- printmakers
- sculptors

Certification and Licensing

Illustrators need to continue their education and training while pursuing their careers. Licensing and certification are not required in this field. However, illustrators must keep up with the latest innovations in design techniques, computer software, and presentation technology, as well as technological advances in the fields for which they provide illustrations.

The Association of Medical Illustrators offers the voluntary Certified Medical Illustrator designation. To be eligible, applicants must graduate from an accredited program or obtain at least five years' experience and complete a course in gross anatomy with hands-on dissection.

Internships and Volunteerships

Internships and volunteerships are a great way to explore this career, and also build up your portfolio. Working under an established illustrator, whether at a newspaper or in an art studio, will allow you to see a professional at work, gain experience and contacts in the industry, and even develop your own skills as an illustrator.

WHO WILL HIRE ME?

More than half of all visual artists are self-employed. Illustrators who are not self-employed work in advertising agencies, design firms, commercial art and reproduction firms, or printing and publishing. They are also employed in the motion picture and television industries, wholesale and retail trade establishments, and public relations firms.

Medical illustrators are employed at hospitals, medical centers, schools, laboratories, pharmaceutical companies, medical and scientific publishers, and advertising agencies. Fashion illustrators are employed at magazines, newspapers, and catalog companies. Cartoonists are employed at magazines, newspapers, publishing houses, and Web design firms.

Aspiring illustrators should develop a portfolio of their work to show to prospective employers or clients. Most schools offer career counseling and job placement assistance to their graduates. Job ads, employment agencies, and direct mail campaigns are also potential methods for locating work. "I used to have a really aggressive direct mail advertising campaign going four to five times a year," Will says. "I also used to buy pages in *Workbook* and *Showcase* regularly. I now find that I can maintain a steady amount of work without spending as much money on advertising. I have worked long enough that much of my early advertising is still working for me. In addition I have a really good [artist] representative, Tammy Shannon, who generates a lot of traffic on her Web site (http://www.shannonassociates.com) as part of a well thought-out marketing plan."

WHERE CAN I GO FROM HERE?

After an illustrator gains experience, he or she will be given more challenging and unusual work. Those with strong computer skills will have the best chances for advancement. Illustrators can advance by developing skills in a specialized area, or even starting their own business. Like Will, illustrators can also go into teaching, in colleges and universities at the post-secondary, undergraduate, and graduate levels.

Will would like to eventually illustrate children's picture books exclusively. "It feels weird to actually be close to my life-long dream," he says. "How many people can say they are doing exactly what they want to be doing? When I'm constantly under contract I don't see myself wanting much more out of my professional life."

WHAT ARE THE SALARY RANGES?

The pay for illustrations can be as little as a byline (a published credit with your name), though in the beginning of your career it may be worth it just to get exposure. Some illustrators can earn several thousand dollars for a single illustration.

The Pros and Cons of Being an Illustrator

Every job has its pros and cons, whether it's a flexible schedule and free coffee or long hours and cramped cubicles. We asked Will Terry what he thought were the best and worst aspects of being a free-lance illustrator, and here's what he said.

Pros

- Watching *Oprah* in your jammies

- Landing projects that pay much more than you could make as an in-house artist.

- Working at odd times to free up time to go snowboarding.

- Being able to make important art deci-sions on some projects.

- Not reporting to the same boss every-day.

- Listening to your music as loud as you want.

- Feeling fulfilled by seeing a dream through to the end.

Cons

- No regular paychecks—sometimes the mailbox holds three months worth of income.

- No benefits—health insurance is very expensive for a family of five like mine, and until a few years ago prior to my wife entering the workforce, we paid about $8,000 a year for premiums and deductibles.

- Having to pay the full 15 percent FICA. If you are working right now examine your pay stub and you'll find that your employer pays 7.5 percent.

- Getting involved in projects that you wish you would have turned down for numerous reasons.

- Running the business side.

- Paying for advertising.

- Working holidays.

Freelance work is often uncertain because of the fluctuation in pay rates and steadiness of work. The U.S. Department of Labor reports that median earnings for salaried fine artists, including painters, sculptors, and illustrators, were $41,280 in 2005. The top 10 percent earned more than $79,950 and the bottom 10 percent earned less than $19,580.

Illustrators generally receive good benefits, including health and life insurance, pension plans, and vacation, sick, and holiday pay. Self-employed illustrators do not typically receive these benefits from their employers. They must pay for their own health insurance and other benefits and cannot count on receiving regular paychecks.

WHAT IS THE JOB OUTLOOK?

Employment of visual artists is expected to grow about as fast as the average for all occupations through 2014, according to the *Occupational Outlook Handbook.* The growth of the Internet should provide opportunities for illustrators, although the increased use of computer-aided design systems is a threat because individuals do not necessarily need artistic talent or training to use them. The Society of Illustrators adds that at this time, the job market for illustrators is competitive because there is a surplus of qualified, talented individuals looking for work.

According to Will, "employment opportunities in illustration are both dismal and exciting! By that I mean this: If you are looking at illustration as a career oppor-

tunity to earn money to support yourself and perhaps a family you'd probably do better to look elsewhere. I think we've reached the point where the money just isn't there for most beginning illustrators, and if you're looking at it from a money standpoint, you're setting yourself up for a big disappointment. However, there is always room at the top. If you are the type of person that is committed, persistent, and full of determination, it is possible for you to find work in just about any area of illustration you choose. Basically you have to be the kind of person who has the art bug so bad that the only remedy is to create and create and market, market, market. When your work comes from your passion you'll find that success and money are a byproduct."

One option to better your chances at finding employment is to specialize. The employment outlook for medical illustrators is very good. Because there are only a few graduate programs in medical illustration with small graduation classes, medical illustrators will find great demand for their skills. The field of medicine and science in general is always growing, and medical illustrators will be needed to depict new techniques, procedures, and discoveries.

The outlook for careers in fashion illustration is dependent on the businesses of magazine publishing and advertising. Growth of advertising and public relations agencies will provide new jobs. The popularity of American fashion in other parts of the world will also create a demand for fashion illustrators to provide the artwork needed to sell to a global market.

Multimedia Artists

SUMMARY

Definition
Multimedia artists create art for commercial and fine art purposes by combining traditional artistic skills with new technologies such as computers, scanners, and digital cameras.

Alternative Job Titles
Artists
Computer artists
Digital artists

Salary Range
$29,000 to $50,000 to $93,000+

Educational Requirements
High school diploma

Certification or Licensing
None available

Employment Outlook
About as fast as the average

High School Subjects
Art
Computer science
History

Personal Interests
Art
Computers
Drawing
Photography

Successful artists are not only good at creating art, but they are also skilled at marketing their work. "I devote many hours each month seeking venues in which to exhibit my work, e-mailing and sending packets of materials through the mail," says Joan Myerson Shrager, a multimedia artist. "When traveling, I make it a point to have professional business cards and an album with a cross section of small prints. You never know which gallery will show interest; therefore it pays to contact as many as possible. Recently, on a trip to Los Angeles, a gallery owner who liked my work, but couldn't use it, referred me to another gallery. I secured an exhibition because of this encounter."

WHAT DOES A MULTIMEDIA ARTIST DO?

Multimedia artists use new technologies to create art for commercial and fine art purposes. Instead of a traditional paintbrush and canvas, they use a mouse, keyboard, scanner, digital camera, and other computer equipment to create their works. Their creations can be seen both in a museum gallery or on commercial-product packaging. They may work as freelance artists, or work in computer and video gaming, advertising, animation, and other diverse industries.

Multimedia artists use their creative abilities and technological skills to produce original works of art to express ideas; to provide social and cultural commentary; to communicate messages; to sell products; to explore color, texture, line, and other visual elements; and for many other purposes.

Many multimedia artists work as self-employed fine artists. They spend years developing their own style, focusing on a chosen subject, and refining their skills with their equipment. Most artists change styles subtly as they gain experience in their art and in their lives, and some experiment with different technology. For example, a multimedia artist may start out using digital photography to create realistic looking images, but might become more experimental over time, manipulating his or her images more for visual effect.

Multimedia fine artists spend a good deal of their time trying to sell their work, searching for appropriate galleries or art shows that fit their work and have decent traffic through them to increase chances for a sale. The gallery owner and artist set the prices for pieces of art, and the gallery owner receives a commission on any work that sells. The relationship between the gallery owner and artist is often one of close cooperation. For example, a gallery owner may encourage artists to explore new techniques, styles, and ideas while helping to establish their reputation. As a multimedia artist becomes well known, selling his or her work often becomes easier, and many well-known artists receive commissions for their art.

Multimedia commercial artists may be employed full time or work contractually in graphic design, advertising, publishing, electronic games, and even the film industry. Their art differs from fine art in that it is usually created according to the wishes of a client or employer. Because computers are now widely used to create illustrations and other visual affects, the technological skills of multimedia artists can be applied almost anywhere in print or online publishing. Artists might create their work on the computer, or more traditional "pen and paper" drawings, paintings, collages, and other two-dimensional pieces can be scanned, digitized, and then manipulated using software programs.

To Be a Successful Multimedia Artist, You Should . . .

- be creative and imaginative
- have a passion for creating art
- be determined and have a thick skin when it comes to the opinions of others
- have well-developed computer skills and knowledge of Adobe Photoshop, Illustrator, or similar programs
- be willing to continue to learn new techniques and technologies
- be disciplined and willing to work constantly on your art to develop your skills and talent
- have excellent communication skills
- have strong business and marketing skills

Multimedia artists are innovators and are not bound by tradition or convention. They respond to cultural and societal stimuli and incorporate them into works of art. In addition to standard computer equipment, they also use copiers and other technology not originally intended for art as alternative media.

WHAT IS IT LIKE TO BE A MULTIMEDIA ARTIST?

Joan Myerson Shrager has been an artist for more than 30 years, but has only focused on computer-based art for the last several years. (To view Joan Myerson Shrager's art, visit http://www.joan-myerson-shrager.com.) "I was a painter using acrylics and mixed media for many years before becoming a digital artist," she says. "I exhibited in more than 75 juried exhibitions and many solo shows." To create digital art, Shrager combines freehand images with photography or uses freehand images alone. "I work directly on the computer to create digital paintings that are multilayered collages," she explains. "The monitor is the canvas and the software functions as palette and tools."

Shrager works in a studio that is set up with a computer, monitor, printers, and an art library. "I find it very important to have enough space—eight to 10 feet—to step away from the large screen. Of course, I do not actually have to be working physically to be creating and conceptualizing. My mind is always processing ideas."

Multimedia artists find many sources of inspiration when creating their art. "Since

I frequently do narrative work," Shrager says, "my ideas come from my interests such as family, current events, etc. Then I begin gathering materials (sketches, photos, artifacts) into the giant sketchbook that is my computer. I collect photographic images and continuously make freehand sketches. For this, the Internet is a tremendous reference library. I also have an extensive personal collection of memorabilia."

Shrager makes many studies for the final work of art. She says that the process takes weeks of formulating and reformulating ideas, many of which she files away for later use. "Sometimes I combine several studies to create one finished product," she says. "The software enables addition and removal of sections so I can evaluate whether the 'painting' is balanced and whether the composition works. As I work, I rotate the image to see it from different perspectives. I change colors and sometimes totally remove colors. I often print small sections that are much enlarged to see the effect on large-scale paper." Shrager spends about five to seven hours a day at the computer while working on a project.

Some multimedia artists teach at the high school and college levels. Jeannie Mecorney is a multimedia art and technology instructor at Cañada College in Redwood City, California. She has been an educator for seven years. Before becoming a teacher, she worked as a graphic designer and a Web and video designer for more than 20 years. "I spend an average of three hours a day in the classroom teaching digital art classes such as Introduction to Computer Graphics, Digital Imaging, Digital Illustration, Digital Painting, Digital Page Layout, Web Design, Web Animation, and Digital Photography and Audio," Jeannie says. She spends the rest of her day advising students regarding their course work or career aspirations and also spends several weeks annually attending workshops, seminars, conventions, and demonstrations of the latest hardware and software. "This industry is constantly changing and improving hardware, software, and peripherals," Jeannie says, "which keeps my job exciting and interesting! Do not enter this field if you want to be doing the same thing year in and year out!"

DO I HAVE I WHAT IT TAKES TO BE A MULTIMEDIA ARTIST?

Like all artists, multimedia artists need creativity, imagination, patience, persistence, determination, independence, and sensitivity. However, unlike other artists, they also need fine computer skills to be able to work with their high-tech tools and canvases. They need working knowledge of several of the common drawing, image editing, and page layout programs, such as Adobe Photoshop or Illustrator. Multimedia art can be created with both Macintosh systems and on PCs; in fact, many artists have both types of computers in their studios.

Artists also need to have confidence in their abilities, but they also need to be realistic about their abilities. "If you are honest with yourself you will learn and grow," Joan Myerson Shrager says. "Never

be satisfied. Being an artist is a calling. Artists are driven to create. Develop a thick skin because there are frequent rejections. Keep on creating! Do not become set in your approach to your art."

Helen Morvasky, a digital artist who creates digitally produced fine art for print, believes that the most important professional qualities for multimedia artists are discipline and the ability to self-start. "Even if you don't feel inspired you should still work on something," she says. "Oftentimes inspiration comes while you are working. If it doesn't you are still exercising your mind and developing and refining your skills." (To view Helen's art, visit http://www.artispictura.com.)

If your interest is in fine art, be prepared to take a second job, especially when you are starting out. With the proper training and educational background, many fine artists are able to work in art-related positions, such as art teachers, art directors, or graphic designers, while pursuing their art activities independently.

HOW DO I BECOME A MULTIMEDIA ARTIST?

Joan Myerson Shrager says that she received her most meaningful training to become a multimedia artist by attending drawing, painting, and sculpture classes in various fine art institutions, including the Moore College of Art and Design, Tyler School of Art, and the University of the Arts in Philadelphia, Pennsylvania. "I am self-taught on the computer with the exception of a few initial basic lessons," she says. "The more I work at it, the more proficient I become. Even after many years I continue to learn new techniques. In the beginning I kept records of almost every step I took on the computer in order to go back and repeat an effect. Now, of course, there are excellent computer art programs offered in art educational institutions."

Helen Moravsky received her B.A. in communications, with honors in visual media, from The American University in Washington, D.C. "My background in film has been the defining part of my experience," she says. "It was an invaluable discipline which gave me a sense of composition, lighting, color, motion, and depth of field. My influences come from film as well as traditional art and they overlap in the areas of German Expressionism and Surrealism. My first introduction to computer graphics was through the experimental films of the Whitney brothers, engineers for IBM who first developed the light pen in the 1960s, and who then produced two films made up of the geometric shapes they were able to achieve through the computer. It was that exposure that began my fascination with digital art."

Education

High School

In the public school system, there is very little art instruction at the elementary level, so high school is your chance to take as many art courses as you can. While you will be specializing in computer-based art, all multimedia artists should have a good foundation in the traditional art disciplines, such as painting, illustration, ceramics, and traditional photography. If your school has computer design or imaging classes, be sure to take those. These classes will give you experience in working with page layout programs and art/photo manipulation programs. Even general computing classes will be useful just to get comfortable with using a computer and different software. Helen Moravsky suggests that high school students who are interested in any part of the digital art field should take at least a preliminary computer programming course. "This gives them grounding for multimedia, Web-based, or animation art," she explains. "If at all possible, students should take a course or do tutorials in Photoshop. It is the preeminent tool that every digital artist must have in their arsenal."

Outside of class, try working on the school newspaper or yearbook staff. This can provide valuable design experience. You could also volunteer to design flyers or posters for school events such as athletic tournaments or plays.

Postsecondary Training

There are no formal educational requirements for becoming a multimedia artist. Some people start out seeking an associate degree in art, and then head out to the job market or start creating on their own. Others pursue a four-year bachelor's of art degree at an art school, general college, or university. Some seek out degrees in computer science, graphic design, or other related field.

Typical classes taken by a multimedia art student include traditional studio art, computer graphics, digital imaging, digital photography, Web design, animation, and digital page layout.

Get Started Now!

It's never too early to begin learning about art. Joan Myerson Shrager offers the following useful suggestions, in her own words, to high school students who are interested in becoming artists:

- Visit galleries.

- Visit artist studio buildings and attend open houses where you can visit and talk with artists.

- Find the local art newspaper, which will be an excellent source of information about what is happening in the art world in your area.

- Seek out cooperative galleries and nonprofit art centers to talk to artists. *Gallery Guide* is usually available for free in most galleries.

- Head to the library. Look at art magazines.

- Check out the Internet for information on art exhibitions.

- Check out local art schools that offer weekend classes for interested students.

- It is often possible to arrange a visit to your local art college. You can probably sit in on actual classes.

- Talk to as many people in the field as you can. Working artists are very different than gallery owners because they are the troops who are producing the work, and they can tell you how hard it is to get your work reviewed by a gallery. In general, it has been my experience that experienced artists are willing to share their thoughts with young or new artists.

- It is very important to explore as many fields connected with art that you can. Being a working artist is much like being an actor. If you are talented and are lucky, you might make a living at it. The likelihood of this happening is very slim, so it would be a good idea to be trained in an allied field like teaching, gallery management, or art administration that allows you to make a living and pursue your dream.

In addition to formal training, Joan Myerson Shrager advises students to create art and learn constantly. "I read the latest magazines both on computer art software and conventional art," she says. "I read the computer literature as well. There is always something new to experiment with."

Certification and Licensing

There is no traditional certification or licensing available for multimedia artists. Artists who sell their work to the pub- lic may have to obtain special permits from their local or state tax office. Artists should also check with the Internal Revenue Service to learn more about tax information related to income received from the sale of artwork.

Internships and Volunteerships

Whatever their educational background, most multimedia artists start out in unpaid internships or volunteerships. These positions are invaluable to gain experience and professional connections. Some art degree programs require an internship for credit, and may assist in finding a position with a local business or organization.

Students in Jeannie Mecorney's program at Cañada College are strongly encouraged to participate in its co-op education program. "Our campus provides units for students who work while going to school through our CoOp Education department," she says. "In addition, we have several industry contacts through our Multimedia Art and Technology Advisory Committee who offer internships at companies such as *Communication Arts Magazine,* Electronic Arts, and PDI/Dreamworks. Local organizations also employ our students on a part-time or project-oriented basis."

WHO WILL HIRE ME?

The majority of multimedia artists are employed on a freelance basis and exhibit or sell their work on their own. Helen Moravsky's work is currently available at her Web site, but she is also in the midst of working with two galleries that are interested in carrying her art. "Finding a gallery is hard work for any artist and particularly so for digital artists," she says. "Digital art is still in its infancy and is having to make inroads into the art establishment." Most established galleries have a stable of artists whose work they carry and they are not in the market for new ones. "Digital artists should look for galleries that take on new and emerging artists," Helen suggests. "If you are able to visit the gallery, take a look at the type of art they present and determine if yours will fit with the overall aesthetic. If you can't go to the gallery, look online. Most galleries have a Web site, and that will help you determine if your work would fit in. Galleries get submissions for review all the time and therefore they have guidelines as to how they wish to see the work (on slides, disc, etc.). If that information is not available on their Web site, then contact them for information. Once you make a submission for review, you should expect to wait at least a couple of months for an answer."

The first and foremost step for a freelance multimedia artist is to develop a portfolio, or a collection of work. The portfolio, which should be organized and showcase a wide variety of the artist's talent and capabilities, is an essential tool when looking for work. Artists just starting out build their portfolio using works created during school, internships and volunteer positions, and then gradually add to it as they gain more on-the-job experience.

Local fairs and art shows often provide opportunities for new artists to display their work. Art councils are a good source of information on upcoming fairs. However, most successful artists are represented by a gallery or agent that displays their work and approaches potential buyers when new works are available. The gallery or agent gets a commission for each piece of artwork sold. Relationships between artists and gallery operators can be tricky, but such relationships can also be beneficial to both creator and seller.

A good gallery operator encourages, supports, and believes in the artists he or she represents.

Many art schools and universities have placement services to help graduates find jobs. Although multimedia artists are generally self-employed, many need to work at another job, at least initially, to support themselves while they establish a reputation.

Some multimedia artists are hired by graphic design firms, advertising agencies, publishing houses, or other businesses. These professionals must also have a strong portfolio. Potential employers rely on portfolios to evaluate talent and how that talent might be used to fit the company's needs.

WHERE CAN I GO FROM HERE?

The channels of advancement for self-employed multimedia artists are not as well defined as they would be for an artist employed at a company. A self-employed artist may become increasingly well known, both nationally and internationally, and may be able to command higher prices for his or her work. The success of an artist depends on a variety of factors, including talent, drive, and determination. However, luck often seems to play a role in many artists' successes, and some artists do not achieve recognition until late in life, if at all. Multimedia artists with business skills may open galleries to display their own and others' work. Those with the appropriate educational backgrounds may become art teachers, agents, writers, or critics.

Commercial multimedia artists can start out in publishing or advertising as graphic designers and with experience become art directors or account executives. As part of their on-the-job training,

Related Jobs

- archivists
- art conservators
- art critics
- art dealers
- art historians
- art teachers
- cartoonists
- ceramic artists
- conservation technicians
- curators
- fashion designers
- fashion illustrators
- gallery directors
- graphic artists
- graphic designers
- illustrators
- memorial designers
- painters
- photo stylists
- photographers
- police artists
- printmakers
- sculptors
- stained glass artists

beginning artists generally are given simpler tasks and work under direct supervision. As they gain experience, they move up to more complex work with increasingly less supervision. Experienced multimedia artists, especially those with leadership capabilities, may be promoted to chief designer or move into other computer-related positions such as graphics programming, animation, or video/computer game design.

WHAT ARE THE SALARY RANGES?

The amount of money earned by multimedia artists varies greatly depending on the industry in which they work. Freelance artists set their own prices depending on the demand for the work. The price they charge is up to them, but much depends on the value the public places on their work. A particular item may sell for a few dollars or tens of thousands of dollars, or at any price in between. The price may increase considerably after it has been sold if the artist's work becomes well known and in demand. According to the U.S. Department of Labor, the median annual earnings of salaried multimedia artists were $50,290 in 2005. Salaries ranged from less than $29,680 to more than $93,060.

Freelance artists often work long hours and earn little, especially when they are first starting out. "Making a living as an artist is difficult unless you are in an area of art with commercial potential," says Joan Myerson Shrager. "Achieving recognition is rare. Deriving satisfaction as

an artist has to be more than expecting to be rewarded."

WHAT IS THE JOB OUTLOOK?

Employment for visual artists, which includes multimedia artists, is expected to grow as fast as the average through 2014, according to the U.S. Department of Labor. However, because they are usually self-employed, much of their success depends on the amount and type of work created, the drive and determination in selling the artwork, and the interest or readiness of the public to appreciate and purchase the work. Continued population growth, higher incomes, and increased appreciation for fine art will create a demand for all visual artists.

Jeannie Mecorney says that the employment outlook is good for multimedia artists. "Many people mistakenly assume that after the dot-com crash, there are no jobs available," she says. "People who have multimedia experience are still able to fill positions in graphic design, Web design, and motion media design. Many companies are still producing newsletters and are in need of corporate design (logos, letterhead, business cards). Companies also need a presence on the Web and use multimedia experts to translate their vision to the Internet. The electronic gaming industry is thriving and currently boasts profits higher than Hollywood!"

Whether working as freelance or commercial artists, multimedia artists should enjoy good employment prospects in coming years as more and more people turn to digital processes as means to communicate and make an artistic expression.

An Interview With Helen Moravsky, Digital Artist

Q. Please describe your work as a multimedia artist. What type of multimedia art do you create?

A. My current work is what is considered digital fine art—digitally produced art intended for print. Over the years I have moved from working in the commercial side of the computer graphics industry to working on my own artistic expression. I started in the computer graphics industry in 1980. At that time the output was limited to transparencies in the form of slides and overheads. Any printing had to be made from those. Virtually all of the work was for corporate presentations—which is still a large part of today's market. As the technology evolved and desktop computers became more sophisticated, I was able to put my experience in film and video to good use in creating multimedia presentations, which included video and audio, for training modules and trade shows.

More recently, I have pursued the creation of my own art and currently create my artworks for output as original prints. The advances in computers, software, printers and inks have made it possible to explore beyond the traditional realms of art into new avenues of expression. What has fascinated me the most is the ability to not just layer images (as one would with collage and montage) but to allow those images to interact with one another, creating a totally new view of reality.

Q. What type of tools/materials do you use to create your art?

A. There are two sets of tools for the digital artist: hardware and software. My hardware consists of a good flat-bed scanner, Mac G4 computer with as much RAM as it will take, a CD/DVD burner, and an Epson 4000 printer (I also have a small desktop printer for just outputting text). As far as software my primary program is Adobe Photoshop. Though there are lots of other programs (many of which I have) that do specific things in given areas.

Q. What are the usual steps that you take to create a work of art?

A. My work is with images. I have collected and continue to collect photographs from the 19th and early 20th centuries. I cull these looking for images that speak to me and that I feel will combine with one another. I usually start with three images, which I have scanned at high resolution and cleaned and corrected as necessary. These form my base. My preference is for albumen photographs (those are the ones that turn into nice sepia tones as they age) because, even faded, they are incredibly rich in detail and depth. Sometimes a particular image will snag my imagination and I can see where I want it to go. Other times the inspiration comes while working and exploring. When I create I limit myself to what the photographs give me. All my textures and features come from within the photographs, they are not added with filters. I begin to layer them, one atop the other, using different compositing methods. Images, or parts of images, are often repeated, added to, or subtracted from to achieve a certain effect.

(continued on next page)

(continued from previous page)

Some of the colors come from the interaction of the images themselves, other color is layered in between to react with the image layers surrounding it. Someone compared my technique to scratch-board, and there is a certain kinship in what I do. My work is as much about what I choose to take out to allow other layers through, as it is about what I add in.

Occasionally, a composition will come together quickly in a few hours. Other times it may take two or three days to find all the right pieces. The time it takes is dictated by the composition, not by my own time clock. When I think I am done with a piece, or if I like it, but am not sure where it is going, I set it aside for a few days or a week and come back to it with a clearer, more detached perspective, looking at it with what one art teacher called "a stranger's eye." When I have determined that a composition is done I flatten the file and go over it in a magnified view, taking out and correcting any lingering problems or things that can only be done in the flattened file rather than the layers until it is where I want it. The final digital steps are setting the levels or curves, the saturation, and sharpening as necessary in preparation for printing. I work at the full size the image is to be printed at—360dpi.

When I determine that the file is ready to print I set my printer file for the proper paper profile and print the first proof. If your monitor is properly calibrated and your printer is printing correctly, your print should look like the screen image. Once the proof is printed I look at it carefully to be certain that there are not problems that show up on the print. If there are, then I determine where the problem is, correct it, and print the next proof until the print is where it should be. The final step is to burn the files onto two discs (making sure to do verification) that act as backup if anything goes wrong with the hard drive.

Q. What are some of the pros and cons of being a multimedia artist?

A. The pros of being a digital artist is that you are on the cutting edge, exploring new realms of expression, doing what you want to do, and most of all creating.

The cons are that, like photography and film before it, digital art has to establish itself with the art world as a legitimate art form. Luckily, this is happening more rapidly with the digital arts because it touches on so many areas. Digital photography, animation, and multimedia are leading the way.

Painters

SUMMARY

Definition
Painters use watercolors, oils, acrylics, and other substances to paint pictures or designs.

Alternative Job Titles
Artists

Salary Range
$19,000 to $41,000 to $79,000+

Educational Requirements
High school diploma

Certification or Licensing
None available

Employment Outlook
About as fast as the average

High School Subjects
Art
History

Personal Interests
Art
Drawing

Working as a painter can be rewarding, challenging, and financially lucrative given the right circumstances—just ask Gayle Hegland.

Last summer, she was commissioned by a prominent local restaurant to paint a large oil painting ("Somer's Bay", 42" x 64") of the expansive beach view of Flathead Lake that could be seen from its upstairs dining room. "The painting was to hang in the entrance and lobby that led up to the main dining room, but had no sight of the shore," she explains. "The owner and I decided on a beautiful summer view of Flathead Lake to remind everyone of that gorgeous season in the Rockies that also happens to be the height of tourist activity."

Gayle began working on the painting in early June and gave herself a one-month deadline to the Fourth of July. "This allowed me time to let each translucent layer of oil glaze dry first before I began another layer," she says. "I also wanted to give the clouds a heavier texture, and this would take time to dry."

Since Gayle prefers to work from life rather than a photo, she was pleased to learn there was a vacant space below the restaurant that had the same view as the proposed painting. As she neared the completion of the painting, she decided to move the painting outside to the shoreline for a more detailed look. "The first day was extremely windy as my painting took on wings and developed a determination

83

to land face down and imprint the texture of the land and sea on its sticky oil surface," she says. "However, it was excellent weather to accurately record the sailboats in motion. The next day, the weather did not fight me. I was positioned on the small area of grass between the shore and the busy highway to get the exact view that I needed."

As Gayle painted, many drivers pulled over to view the same scene on the canvas that they saw from their cars. "Although it is always a bit distracting to be disturbed while painting," she says, "one passerby gave me another commission and, by coincidence, the local newspaper photographer happened by to take my photo. The large photo of my painting and me that was shown in the newspaper, along with its recognition by a former student, led to my next viable commercial mural commission."

WHAT DOES A PAINTER DO?

Painters use their creative abilities to produce original works of art, such as portraits, landscapes, still-lifes, abstracts, and other subjects. They use brushes, palette knives, and other artist's tools to apply color to canvas or other surfaces. Painters are generally classified as fine artists rather than commercial artists because they are responsible for selecting the theme, subject matter, and medium of their artwork.

Painters work in a variety of media, including oil paint, acrylic paint, tempera, watercolors, pen and ink, pencil, charcoal, crayon, and pastels, but may also use such nontraditional media as earth, clay, cement, paper, cloth, and any other material that allows them to express their artistic ideas. Painters develop line, space, color, and other visual elements to produce the desired effect. They may prefer a particular style of art, such as realism or abstract, and they may be identified with a certain technique or subject matter. Many artists develop a particular style and apply that style across a broad range of techniques, from painting to etching to sculpture.

As film, video, and computer technology have developed, the work of painters has expanded into new forms of expression. Three-dimensional computer animation techniques in particular often blur the boundaries between painting, photography, and cinema.

WHAT IS IT LIKE TO BE A PAINTER?

Gayle Hegland is a painter in Lakeside, Montana. Her work has been exhibited throughout the United States and the world. "Being a painter," she says, "allows you to be able to do what you enjoy and are good at, establish your own hours most of the time, and express yourself like in few other professions."

In addition to working as a painter, Gayle teaches at Flathead Valley Community College and is well-known for her illustrations that have appeared in publications such as *Sports Illustrated, Condé Nast Traveler, The National Law Journal, The New York Times,* and *The Chronicle of Higher Education.* (To view Gayle's work

---

Painting Glossary

broken color Colors laid next to each other and blended by the eye of the viewer; thus instead of mixing red and blue on a palette to produce purple, red and blue are placed next to each other on the canvas

drybrush A technique in which paint of a thick consistency is stroked lightly over a dry surface; it produces a broken or mottled effect

glaze A film of transparent paint applied over a solid color, producing a luminous, rich effect

grisaille A monochromatic painting, usually in shades of gray; it may be a finished painting or an underpainting

impasto A thick application of paint to a canvas or panel; the marks of the brush or palette knife can be seen plainly

imprimatura A toned ground created by a thin wash or glaze of transparent color

scumble An application of opaque paint over a different color of paint; the original color is not covered entirely, giving an uneven effect

stippling The technique of applying small dots of paint to a surface to build up tonal areas or textures

underpainting A preliminary painting on the painting surface; using tones of one color, the artist makes an underpainting to establish the basic shapes, values, and overall composition of a painting

wash A thin layer of paint spread evenly over a broad area

wet-in-wet A technique in which fresh paint is applied on top of or into wet paint already on the support; used with watercolors and oils and can produce both distinctive contrasts of color and softly blended effects

---

as a fine artist and illustrator, visit http://mail.fvcc.edu/~ghegland and http://www.illustratorspartnership.org.)

Many artists work in studios, often separate from their homes, where they can produce their work in privacy and quiet. Some painters, however, work outdoors. Most artists combine both indoor and outdoor work during their careers. "My father built a studio and apartment for me [in my parents'] house's walk-out lower level on our 40 acres in the Montana Rockies by Flathead Lake," Gayle says. "This was in the late '80s and he, being a former railroad man, filled it with Northern Pacific railroad memorabilia that he had collected. He used old snow board fence for paneling long before 'distressed' wood was fashionable. Because I regularly work in oils, in the summer I also love to work outside under a gazebo and leave my work there to dry between glazes."

Every painter has his or her own way of working and finding inspiration. Some painters may choose complete solitude in order to work and be inspired; others thrive on interaction with other artists and people. Some artists may view and study famous works of art, read a book, take a walk, or do a variety of other activities to become inspired. For her own projects, Gayle says that she "doesn't often need inspiration if I have the idea since technique, or theory, backs this up. I always want to take much longer on some personal projects than for the typical client deadline." But if she is creating a work of art on commission, the client almost always inspires the idea. "I usually start with sketches, particularly if I need a client's OK to go ahead with an idea," she says. "If I do need inspiration, I will look at a favorite artist's work, see a movie on the subject, do Internet research, or read a book. For a commission, I often must work very fast depending on the client situation, the amount of time I am allowed to stay somewhere for research, or as in the case of flowers, an occurrence like a sunrise, or a person, it's life span, growth, change, or access."

When Gayle is not painting, teaching, or preparing her lessons, she keeps very busy promoting her work, studying new concepts to paint, exploring grant applications, talking to clients, negotiating contracts, preparing taxes, and handling other business concerns. She also travels for research, training, and conventions; to study new ideas, cultures, or artists; to visit museums; and to promote her work in person to old and new clients alike.

Painters often work long hours, and those who are self-employed do not receive paid vacations, insurance coverage, or any of the other benefits usually offered by a company or firm. However, these painters are able to work at their own pace, own and manage their copyrights, set their own prices, and make their own decisions. The energy and creativity that go into an artist's work brings feelings of pride and satisfaction. Most artists genuinely love what they do.

DO I HAVE WHAT IT TAKES TO BE A PAINTER?

In order to be a painter, you must have artistic ability. Of course, this is entirely

To Be a Successful Painter, You Should . . .

- have artistic ability and a passion for creating art

- have a strong belief in your artistic abilities and potential

- be willing to work very hard to develop a reputation in the field

- be able to handle occasional criticism of your work

- have an excellent imagination and a willingness to try new techniques and styles

- have strong communication skills, especially when dealing with customers, art dealers, and gallery directors

- have strong business and marketing skills

subjective, and it is perhaps more important that you believe in your own ability and in your own potential. "Being an artist is a very difficult life," Gayle says, "and it is quite possible that you will forever lead a life of obscurity and never be appreciated or 'discovered'. Especially if you are poor, you must have the passion or confidence in the area to sustain you and then possibly you will reap the benefits of maturity."

Apart from being creative, imaginative and persistent, you should be patient, independent, and sensitive. Gayle says it also helps to have an extremely thick skin since your work will be critiqued and at times unfairly commented upon by potential buyers, gallery owners, and others. You will also need to be good at business and sales if you intend to support yourself through your art. As a small businessperson, you must be able to market and sell your paintings to wholesalers, retailers, and the general public.

There is no single way to become or to be an artist. As with other areas of the arts, painting is an intensely personal endeavor. If it is possible to generalize, most painters are people with a desire and need to visually explore and record or express the world around them or the world within them, or both. Throughout their careers, they seek to develop their vision and the methods and techniques that allow them to best express themselves. Many painters work within a tradition, genre, or style of art. They may develop formal theories of art or advance new theories. Painters are usually aware of the art that has come before them as well as the work of the current day.

HOW DO I BECOME A PAINTER?

Art has played a significant role in Gayle's family for generations. "My grandmother [well-known portrait and landscape artist Elessa Manley] started me painting very early because she recognized that I had talent, potential, and a similar vision to hers," Gayle says. "My parents were first-generation immigrants and had a strong belief in the benefits of a higher education. It also was an acceptable profession, by my family, for me to be an artist and a professor at a college. I stayed in school a long time and received my B.F.A. in studio fine art and an M.A. in studio fine art from the University of Montana-Missoula and, because I was primarily a figurative and narrative artist, an M.F.A. in both studio fine art and illustration from the School of Visual Arts in New York City, . . . My M.F.A. virtually showed me that there was little difference between fine art and great illustration other than the means of display and audience."

Education

High School

There are no specific educational requirements for becoming a painter. However, several high school classes can help you prepare for a career in this field, including art and history. Take many kinds of art classes to learn different techniques and styles, and determine which you excel at. "For the beginning artist and student," Gayle says, "I highly recommend they work on something that they have a passion for. A favorite subject can give the beginning artist the 'inspiration' that can give them the interest and get them on the right track to learn about theory and technique." Business and finance classes may also be beneficial, since you will likely have to manage your own financial transactions as a painter.

Gayle also recommends that students participate in summer programs that help them develop their artistic ability and interest. "During my summers in high school," she says, "I attended a college summer theatre program at Moorhead State University in Minnesota, where I was given great creative visual opportunities and exposure that encouraged me to be very confident in my visual skills."

Postsecondary Training

Although there isn't a clear path to success in this field, most artists benefit from training, and many attend art schools or programs in colleges and universities. There are also many workshops and other ways for artists to gain instruction, practice, and exposure to art and the works and ideas of other artists. You should learn a variety of techniques, be exposed to as many media and styles as possible, and gain an understanding of the history of art and art theory. By learning as much as possible, you'll be better able to choose the appropriate means for your own artistic expression.

Thousands of colleges offer degrees in the fine arts. According to a 2003 study from *U.S. News & World Report*, some of the top colleges offering degrees in the fine arts include (in alphabetical order):

Atlanta College of Art (http://www.aca.edu), Maine College of Art (http://www.meca.edu), San Francisco Art Institute (http://www.sfai.edu), School of the Art Institute of Chicago (http://www.artic.edu/saic), and the University of the Arts (PA) (http://www.uarts.edu).

Certification and Licensing

Painters who sell their works to the public may need special permits from the local or state tax office. In addition, painters should check with the Internal Revenue Service for laws on selling and tax information related to income received from the sale of artwork. Many artists join professional organizations, such as ArtNetwork, that provide informative advice and tips as well as opportunities to meet with other artists. Gayle is a general member in the Illustrators' Partnership of America. "As an artist," she advises, "I would encourage membership in local museums and anywhere you can be around true professionals that have integrity and want the best for the industry and it's future. Stay away from stockhouses and people who want your copyrights without compensation. They will be the death of your career and the ability to make a living in the industry. It is in my belief system to try to make a contribution to the growth of my industry and fellow artists, rather than to exploit it by tearing at the fabric of the industry's well being. The ability to be able to make a living in the art world is like being able to drink water from a well: The source needs to be respected and not misused, overdrawn, or drained."

Related Jobs

- archivists
- art conservators
- art critics
- art dealers
- art historians
- art teachers
- cartoonists
- ceramic artists
- conservation technicians
- curators
- fashion designers
- fashion illustrators
- gallery directors
- graphic artists
- illustrators
- memorial designers
- multimedia artists
- photo stylists
- photographers
- police artists
- printmakers
- sculptors
- stained glass artists

Internships and Volunteerships

Experience in drawing, painting, and even sculpting can be had at a very early age, even before formal schooling begins. Aspiring painters and sculptors can undertake a variety of artistic projects at school or at home. Additionally, art associations offer beginning classes in various types of art for the general public and there are usually private lessons available that are offered in your area by local accomplished artists.

Contact your local art museums to see about volunteer or internship opportunities. Even if the position is something seemingly unrelated such as giving guided tours, you can still gain valuable knowledge about famous works of art and make contacts in the industry.

WHO WILL HIRE ME?

Because earning a living as a fine artist is very difficult, especially when one is just starting out, many painters work at another job. With the proper training and educational background, many painters are able to work in art-related positions as art teachers, art directors, illustrators, or graphic designers, while pursuing their own art activities independently. For example, many art teachers hold classes in their own studios.

Painters creating large works, such as murals placed outdoors and in public areas, usually work under contract or commission. Most artists, however, create works that express their personal artistic vision and then hope to find someone to purchase them.

WHERE CAN I GO FROM HERE?

Because most painters are self-employed, advancement opportunities are not as well defined as they are at a company or firm.

Artists, Take Your Copyrights Seriously!

Many artists immersed in the creation of their art don't stop to think about the legal aspects of preserving and perpetuating their livelihood. According to Gayle Hegland, "registering and managing one's own copyrights successfully contributes in a very large way to an artist's worth and ability to maintain and build a livelihood." She recommends that artists register all of their original work at the U.S. Copyright Office. She also says that copyrights can provide additional and future income. "They can contribute to a pension plan and be particularly valuable when your technical skills start to deteriorate with age or you are unable to create more original artwork," she explains. "Additionally, the copyrights of your estate, if used correctly, could benefit surviving family members after your death. By retaining and valuing your copyrights you can make additional income through the marketing of editions and signed prints of originals that have long been sold or lost.

"Artists in the United States have not had their right to copyright for very long (1976). It is possible that this right could be taken away if it is not used properly and protected by the intended creator and benefactor. For the benefit of the artist and industry, copyrights should not be taken lightly and should not be given away or sold for some small profit, particularly to stockhouses. Financially desperate and naïve young artists are being bombarded and pressured by stockhouses to sell all their copyrights and future copyrights for a relatively small lump sum. What results is that all their work that has been bought up by these large, nonartist-owned stockhouses actually makes that same artist compete financially in their market against themselves. It also causes a ripple effect that brings . . . the monetary value of art as an investment down for all artists."

For more information on copyrighting your art, visit http://www.copyright.gov.

A painter may become increasingly well known, both nationally and internationally. As the painter's reputation increases, he or she can command higher prices for work. The success of the fine artist depends on a variety of factors, including talent, drive, and determination. However, luck often seems to play a role in many painters' success, and some individuals do not achieve recognition until late in life, if at all. Painters with business skills may open their own galleries or create online galleries to display and sell their own and others' work. Those with the appropriate educational backgrounds may become art teachers, agents, or critics.

"I would like to continue my development as an artist," Gayle says, "and, by doing so, make a contribution to my industry, the community, and to my family."

WHAT ARE THE SALARY RANGES?

The amount of money earned by visual artists varies greatly. More than 50 percent are self-employed—a figure that is more than five times greater than other occupations. As freelancers, painters can set their hours and prices. Those employed by businesses usually work for the motion picture and television industries, wholesale or retail trades, publishing companies, or public relations firms.

According to the U.S. Department of Labor, the median annual salary for fine artists, including painters, sculptors, and illustrators, was $41,280 in 2005. Earn $19,580 to $79,950 or more. Some internationally known artists may command millions of dollars for their work.

Painters often work long hours and earn little, especially when they are first starting out. "Even if you are shrewd or good at making money, finances are always a concern even when you become established," Gayle advises. The price artists charge is up to them, but much depends on the value the public places on their work. A particular painting may sell for a few dollars or tens of thousands of dollars, or at any price in between. Often, the value of a painting may increase considerably after it has been sold. A painting that may have earned an artist only a few hundred dollars may earn many thousands of dollars the next time it is sold.

Some painters obtain grants that allow them to pursue their art; others win prizes and awards in competitions. Most painters, however, have to work on their projects part time while holding down a regular, full-time job. Many artists teach in art schools, high schools, or out of their studios. Painters who sell their work must pay Social Security and other taxes on any money they receive.

WHAT IS THE JOB OUTLOOK?

Employment for visual artists is expected to grow about as fast as the average for all occupations through 2014, according to the U.S. Department of Labor. Because they are often self-employed, much of painters' success depends on the amount and type of work created, the drive and determination to sell their artwork, and the interest or readiness of the public to appreciate and purchase their work. Population growth, higher incomes, and increased appreciation for fine art will create a demand for visual artists, but competition for positions in this field will be keen.

Success for a painter is difficult to quantify. Individual painters may consider themselves successful as their talent matures and they are better able to present their vision in their work. This type of success goes beyond financial considerations. Few artists enter this field for the money. Financial success depends on a great deal of factors, many of which have nothing to do with the artist or his or her work. Painters with good marketing skills will likely be the most successful in selling their work. Although artists should not let their style be dictated by market trends, those interested in financial success can attempt to determine what types of artwork the public wants.

It often takes several years for an artist's work and reputation to be established. Many painters have to support themselves through other employment. There are numerous employment opportunities for commercial artists in such fields as publishing, advertising, fashion and design, and teaching. Painters should consider employment in these and other fields. They should be prepared, however, to face strong competition from others who are attracted to these fields.

Photographers

SUMMARY

Definition
Photographers take, develop, and print pictures of people, places, objects, and events, using a variety of cameras and photographic equipment.

Alternative Job Titles
Artist

Salary Range
$15,000 to $26,000 to $53,000+

Educational Requirements
Some postsecondary training

Certification or Licensing
None available

Employment Outlook
About as fast as the average

High School Subjects
Art
Business
Chemistry
Computer science

Personal Interests
Art
Photography

Theresa Bertocci has truly come to love Adobe Photoshop, one of the electronic tools that has profoundly changed the field of photography over the last several years.

The Chicago-based photographer was on location, shooting a series of portraits at a remote site. "I had set up a temporary studio in a high school classroom using portable strobe (studio flash) lighting and a large, sweeping white backdrop," she recalls. "I had strategically positioned the lighting and carefully metered the first subject to ensure that my camera was set correctly to expose the film properly. Because all of the subjects throughout the day were to be positioned at the exact same spot using the exact same lighting, to save time I did not re-meter each subject."

Theresa didn't realize until a few days later—and after the film was processed—that someone had moved one of the studio light stands during the shoot, causing the last few portraits of the day to be severely underexposed on one side. "Because re-shooting the portraits was not an option," she says, "I decided to try to salvage the work digitally. I scanned the medium-format negatives (using a film scanner) into my computer and used Photoshop to carefully and selectively brighten the dark areas and fine-tune the final images.

"While a few years ago, a photographer might have had to admit the mistake to the client and junked the negatives, digital darkroom techniques allowed me to salvage the job."

WHAT DOES A PHOTOGRAPHER DO?

Photography is both an artistic and technical occupation. There are many variables in the process that a knowledgeable *photographer* can manipulate to produce a clear image or a more abstract work of fine art. First, photographers know how to use cameras and can adjust the focus, shutter speeds, aperture, lenses, and filters. They know about the types and speeds of films. Photographers also know about light and shadow, deciding when to use available natural light and when to set up artificial lighting to achieve desired effects.

Some photographers send their film to laboratories, but some develop their own negatives and make their own prints. These processes require knowledge about chemicals such as developers and fixers and how to use enlarging equipment. Photographers must also be familiar with the large variety of papers available for printing photographs, all of which deliver a different effect. Most photographers continually experiment with photographic processes to improve their technical proficiency or to create special effects.

Digital photography, while a relatively new development, has revolutionized the way people take, print, and share pho-

tographs. With this new technology, film is replaced by microchips that record pictures in digital format. Pictures can then be downloaded onto a computer's hard drive. Photographers use special software to manipulate the images on screen. Though some photographers sill use traditional cameras and film, the majority of professional photographers now use digital equipment to take, manipulate, and send photos.

Photographers usually specialize in one of several areas: fine art, portraiture, commercial and advertising photography, photojournalism, educational photography, and scientific photography are just a few examples. There are subspecialties within each of these categories. A *scientific photographer,* for example, may specialize in aerial or underwater photography. A *commercial photographer* may specialize in food or fashion photography.

Some photographers write for trade and technical journals, teach photography in schools and colleges, act as representatives of photographic equipment manufacturers, sell photographic equipment and supplies, produce documentary films, or do freelance work.

A photographer's work conditions vary based on the job and employer. Commercial and portrait photographers work in comfortable surroundings, spending most of their time in a studio. Photojournalists seldom are assured physical comfort in their work and may face danger when covering stories on natural disasters or military conflicts. Some photographers work in research laboratory settings; others work on aircraft; and still others work underwater. For some photographers, conditions change from day to day. One day, they may be photographing a hot and dusty rodeo; the next they may be taking pictures of a dogsled race in Alaska.

WHAT IS IT LIKE TO BE A PHOTOGRAPHER?

Because Theresa Bertocci does both commercial and art-focused photography work, she works in a variety of environments. "I have a small indoor portrait studio where I take portraits of individuals and small groups," she says. "I also do some location work, which can either be indoors (e.g., hotel conferences, clients' homes) or outdoors (location portraits, architectural photographs, nature photography). Because I process most of my work digitally, I spend a *lot* of time indoors, in my digital darkroom (and I mean *dark*)."

When asked about primary and secondary duties as a photographer, Theresa stresses that it can be dangerous to categorize her job duties as primary and secondary, "because that creates a situation where some of the duties rarely—or never—get done! With that said, most photographers, myself included, tend to think of shooting and printing photographs as primary, and the business and administrative duties such as estimating, billing, marketing, preparing/obtaining signatures on forms (e.g., model or property releases), continuing education, backing-up/archiving files, and research (e.g., art fairs in which to exhibit and stock photo agencies to carry their work) as secondary."

Many photographers work a 35- to 40-hour workweek, but freelancers and news photographers often put in long, irregular hours on a variety of tasks. "The time that I spend taking photographs—versus processing and printing photographs, versus administrative duties—varies by the type of photographic work being done, whether it is film- or digital-based photography, and how much of the work is outsourced by the photographer," Theresa says. "I am a sole proprietor and have my own digital darkroom, and I rarely outsource any processing or printing, including proof sheets. Consequently, I probably spend about 10 percent of my time each month shooting photographs, 30 percent processing and printing, and the rest on other duties. As with most sole proprietors, more often than not, the duties that appear last in my 'to do' list never get done at all; therefore it is critical for photographers to properly prioritize their duties."

Fine art photographers may have the luxury of taking shots for art's sake, but must worry about the market for their work. The lucky few might get a chance to have their work shown in an art gallery, but most others sell their work through word of mouth or by displaying works on a personal Web site. "Photographers who are trying to make a living (as opposed to a hobby) at photography usually have to work in more than one photography arena to support themselves," Theresa says. "Photographers often take on freelance or commercial jobs to support their

To Be a Successful Photographer, You Should . . .

● ● ● ● ● ● ● ●

- have manual dexterity, good eyesight, and strong color vision

- have artistic ability

- have an eye for form and line, an appreciation of light and shadow, and the ability to use imaginative and creative approaches to photographs or film

- be patient in order to be able to get just the right effect or shot when taking a photograph

- have strong business and marketing skills

- stay up-to-date regarding the newest technologies

- be creative

- have strong communication skills

the ability to use imaginative and creative approaches to photographs or film, especially in commercial work. In addition, you should be patient and accurate and enjoy working with detail.

Famous Photographers on the Web

Ansel Adams
http://www.pbs.org/wgbh/amex/ansel

Richard Avedon
http://www.richardavedon.com

Harry Callahan
http://www.masters-of-photography
.com/C/callahan/callahan.html

Henri Cartier-Bresson
http://www.henricartierbresson.org/
index_en.htm

Imogen Cunningham
http://www.imogencunningham.com

Dorothea Lange
http://www.getty.edu/art/collections/
bio/a1692-1.html

Annie Leibovitz
http://www.nytimes.com/library/
photos/leibovitz/bourgeois.html

Steichen
http://www.masters-of-photography
.com/S/steichen/steichen_selfportrait_
full.html

Alfred Stieglitz
http://www.pbs.org/wnet/american
masters/database/stieglitz_a.html

Paul Strand
http://www.temple.edu/photo/photo
graphers/strand/strandindex.html

William Wegman
http://www.wegmanworld.com

'habit' of art photography. I think it's a mistake for an art-focused photographer to turn down commercial work, because I have often found that commercial jobs yield ideas or photographs that can later take on a second life as art."

DO I HAVE I WHAT IT TAKES TO BE A PHOTOGRAPHER?

You should possess manual dexterity, good eyesight and color vision, and artistic ability to succeed in this line of work. You need an eye for form and line, an appreciation of light and shadow, and

Theresa believes that successful photographers need to be "creative, self-directed, flexible, and resourceful (to find answers to the business questions such as pricing, which they don't teach you in college). You should also have good interpersonal skills—meaning the ability to work well with people you might find yourself working for, as well as subjects you will be working with at the other end of your lens."

Self-employed (freelance) photographers need good business skills. They must be able to manage their own studios, including hiring and managing assistants and other employees, keeping records, and maintaining photographic and business files. Marketing and sales skills are also important for a successful freelance photographer.

HOW DO I BECOME A PHOTOGRAPHER?

Education

High School

While in high school, take as many art classes and photography classes as are available. Chemistry is useful for understanding the developing and printing processes. You can learn about photo manipulation software and digital photography in computer classes. "Today's photography students," Theresa advises, "*must* incorporate knowledge of Photoshop into their portfolio if they wish to work (even if only part time) in a commercial photography environment. Various organizations offer evening and weekend Photoshop classes. Search the Internet,

yellow pages, or local newspapers to find classes in your area." Additionally, business classes will help if you are considering a freelance career.

Although most colleges that offer degrees in photography plan a curriculum that starts with the basics, you will definitely be more prepared if you obtain some experience in photography before you go to college. Theresa suggests that high school students get involved in taking photographs for their student newspaper or yearbook. "Students can learn how to use 35mm cameras manually to produce interesting photographic effects by taking evening or weekend classes from local park districts, camera stores, and junior colleges," she says. "Taking classes in art history is also critical to developing an artistic 'eye' that can help you develop photographic art that can stand out among traditional art forms such as painting and sculpture." Theresa also stresses the importance of developing your writing skills. "Most fine art photographers who submit their work for consideration must describe in writing the techniques they use and philosophies they hold when creating their art," she explains.

Postsecondary Training

Formal educational requirements depend upon the nature of the photographer's specialty. For instance, photographic work in scientific and engineering research generally requires an engineering background with a degree from a reputable college or institute. Someone who is interested in creating photographic art might major in photography or visual arts.

A college education is not required to become a photographer, although college training probably offers the most promising assurance of success in fields such as industrial, news, or scientific photography. There are degree programs at the associate's, bachelor's, and master's levels. Many schools offer courses in cinematography, although very few have programs leading to a degree in this specialty. Many men and women, however, become photographers with no formal education beyond high school.

After practicing as an "advanced amateur" photographer, as she calls herself, for a number of years, Theresa formally studied photography and obtained a B.A. from Columbia College in Chicago. "I also have taken a number of seminars in digital photography and digital image processing through organizations such as the National Association of Photoshop Professionals," she says. "Because the photography world is continuing to evolve from a primarily film-based environment to a digital capture–based one, ongoing education in digital photographic capture and processing is critical to any photographer who intends to incorporate at least some freelance or commercial work into their business."

To become a photographer, you should have a broad technical understanding of photography and as much practical experience with cameras as possible. Take many different kinds of photographs with a variety of cameras and subjects. Learn how to develop photographs and, if possible, build your own darkroom or rent one. Gain experience in picture composition, cropping prints (cutting images to a desired size), enlarging, and retouching.

Knowledge of digital photography and the software used to manipulate, store, and print images is also highly recommended, if not a necessity, for securing work as a photographer. College classes in computer imaging in addition to studio art and photography are increasingly useful.

Internships and Volunteerships

Some photographers enter the field as apprentices, trainees, or assistants. Trainees may work in a darkroom, camera shop, or developing laboratory. Assistants learn to mix chemicals, develop film, and print photographs, and acquire the other skills necessary to run a portrait or commercial photography business. They may move lights and arrange backgrounds for a commercial or portrait photographer or motion picture photographer. Assistants spend many months learning this kind of work before they move into a job behind a camera.

WHO WILL HIRE ME?

Theresa found her first job in the field with the help of her career counselor at her college. "I worked as an assistant in a portrait studio," she says. "My duties included filing and organizing photographic negatives and prints, trimming photographs to frameable sizes, hand-spotting photographs (to correct print blemishes), digitally retouching images in Photoshop, packaging and mailing customer orders, answering phones, assisting the photographer in the studio and on location (setting up studio lights and

Related Jobs

- agricultural photographers
- archivists
- art conservators
- art critics
- art dealers
- art historians
- art teachers
- artists
- biomedical photographers
- camera operators
- cinematographers and directors of photography
- conservation technicians
- curators
- food photographers
- gallery directors
- graphic designers
- photo editors
- photo stylists
- photographic equipment technicians
- photographic laboratory workers
- photography instructors
- photography store managers and workers
- photojournalists
- sports photographers
- wedding photographers

backdrops, holding reflective bounce cards, making sure the flash is going off), and backing up computer-based photographic digital files."

Approximately 130,000 photographers work in the United States, more than half of whom are self-employed. Most jobs for photographers are provided by photographic or commercial art studios; other employers include newspapers and magazines, radio and TV broadcasting, government agencies, and manufacturing firms. Colleges, universities, and other educational institutions employ photographers to prepare promotional and educational materials and educate students about photography.

WHERE CAN I GO FROM HERE?

Because photography is such a diversified field, there is no typical way in which to get ahead. Those who begin by working for someone else may advance to owning their own businesses. Commercial photographers may gain prestige as more of their pictures are placed in well-known trade journals or popular magazines. Press photographers may advance in salary and the kinds of important news stories assigned to them. A few photographers may become celebrities in their own right by making contributions to the art world or the sciences.

WHAT ARE THE SALARY RANGES?

The U.S. Department of Labor reports that salaried photographers earned median annual salaries of $26,100 in 2005. Salaries ranged from less than $15,240 to more than $53,900. Photographers earned the following mean annual salaries in 2005 by industry: newspaper, book, and directory publishers, $37,230; radio and television broadcasting, $36,100; and colleges and universities, $38,590.

Self-employed photographers often earn more than salaried photographers, but their earnings depend on general business conditions. In addition, self-employed photographers do not receive the benefits that a company provides its employees.

Scientific photographers, who combine training in science with photographic expertise, usually start at higher salaries than other photographers. They also usually receive consistently larger advances in salary than do others, so that their income, both as beginners and as experienced photographers, places them well above the average in their field. Photographers in salaried jobs usually receive benefits such as paid holidays, vacations, sick leave, and medical insurance.

For freelance photographers, the cost of equipment can be quite expensive, with no assurance that the money spent will be repaid through income from future assignments. Freelancers in travel-related photography, such as travel and tourism photographers and photojournalists, have the added cost of transportation and accommodations.

WHAT IS THE JOB OUTLOOK?

Theresa says that the market for corporate/business photography is shrinking. "The digital photography 'revolution' is changing the nature of the photography business," she explains. Many consumers and small business owners are finding it easier—and more affordable—to take and process their own digital images. Also, as mergers and layoffs continue and budgets are cut, the money allocated for projects such as photography, which are perceived as noncritical to business, are being slashed."

Theresa predicts a much more promising future for fine art photography. "On the 'photography as art' side, the market is actually growing," she says. "In recent years, photography has gained respect and become more widely accepted as original 'art.' As photography has become more prominently displayed in important art galleries, it has begun to command prices similar to traditional art such as painting and sculpture."

Photography is a highly competitive field. There are far more photographers than positions available. Only those who are extremely talented and highly skilled can support themselves as self-employed photographers. Many photographers take pictures as a sideline while working another job. Overall, employment of photographers will increase about as fast as the average for all occupations through 2014, according to the *Occupational Outlook Handbook*.

SECTION 3

Do It Yourself

"What are you going to do with your life?" You've probably been asked that question countless times by your friends and family. Since you are reading this book, it is obvious that you are interested in art, but are you aware of all the career options available to you (and the ways to learn more about them)? In addition to pursuing a creative career in painting, photography, or ceramic art, there are options for those who want to help the mentally or physically ill (art therapy), teach art or art history (art education), buy and sell art (gallery ownership and management), restore art (art conservation), and work in many other areas.

No matter what career you're interested in, you are probably already painting, drawing, sculpting, throwing clay, or immersing yourself in the creation of art. That's a great start, but not the only way to learn more about art careers. You probably have never stopped to think of all the different ways you can learn more about art careers while you are still in high school. The following section provides tips on how to learn more about art through hands-on experience. After reading through these suggestions, you'll probably think of even more ways to learn about art. The key is to get cracking now while you're in high school so that you're ready to enter the field or pursue a college education in the arts after you graduate.

❏ WHAT CAN YOU DO?

Get Your Hands Dirty and Create Art

The best way to learn about anything is by doing, so get going and create some art.

Paint a picture. Sketch your best friend, a pretty flower, or a historic building in your neighborhood. Experiment by taking black and white photographs. Learn to manipulate images in Photoshop. Create a wood or rock sculpture. Throw some clay and create ceramic art. You get the idea. Don't be afraid to try something new or make mistakes. That's the only way you'll learn about art and hone your talents.

Take Art and Related Classes

Take as many art classes as you can in high school, such as painting, drawing, ceramics, sculpture, photography, fibers, computer art, or another specialty. If your high school doesn't offer a good selection of art classes, take a class at your local community center. The key is to keep learning and trying out new mediums, styles, and techniques until you discover your skills and interests. In addition to art classes, you should also take courses in graphic design and computer science since artists are increasingly using computers to create, market, and sell their artwork.

What if you're interested in art, but plan to pursue a career in a nonartistic area of the field? Then be sure to take at least some creative art classes, but augment your art studies with courses in art history, business, marketing, mathematics, and psychology. If you're interested in art conservation, you should take chemistry classes. If you see yourself becoming an art therapist, then take health and psychology courses. If you envision yourself as an art writer, take English and writing classes. You get the idea!

Read Books and Periodicals

Your high school or school library contains a wealth of books and periodicals about art careers, competitions, famous artists, art movements, the arts through history, and the list goes on and on. For a great list of books and periodicals about art, check out Section 4, "What Can I Do Right Now?"

Visit a Museum

Many cities and towns have art museums where you can view art and participate in outreach programs. Ask your art teacher to arrange a field trip to the museum. Of course, you can always visit on your own or with some friends on a weekend or day off.

Some of the larger museums, such as the Los Angeles County Museum of Art (http://www.lacma.org), offer after-school programs that teach high school students about art and allow them to participate in gallery activities and art workshops. Other museums, such as The Museum of Modern Art (http://www.moma.org/education/internships_high.html) in New York City, have teen volunteer programs in which qualified teens intern at the museum in the spring and summer. This is a great way to get involved in the museum, really learn a subject, and meet people in the industry.

This brings up an interesting point: Not many people stop and think about where they want to work. An art museum is a great starting point for career exploration. Some of the most popular positions at museums include museum director, curator, exhibit preparator, art historian, art conservator and restorer, art educator, art librarian, and many other fascinating options.

In addition to visiting a museum, you can also become a member for a relatively small fee. Membership benefits vary by institution, but most include the opportunity to view special exhibitions in advance of the general public, invitations to free lectures about art, and discounts at museum shops and facilities.

Surf the Web

If you can't easily visit an art museum or gallery, the Internet is one of the next best tools for exploration. In addition to viewing online archives of amazing and groundbreaking art, you can surf the Web to find art museums, galleries, associations, discussion groups, competitions, educational programs, glossaries, company information, artist profiles and interviews, and much more. To help get you started, we've prepared a list of what we think are the best art sites on the Web. Check out Section 4, "What Can I Do Right Now?," for more info.

Join a Club

Want to immerse yourself in art and meet like-minded people? Then join an art or photography club. Most junior high and high schools have art or photography clubs that meet after school—or maybe your local community organization (such as the YMCA) offers such a club. As a member of an art or photography club, you might learn how to improve your oil painting techniques or how to use a digital camera, listen to a lecture by a well-known artist, tour a local art gallery or museum, participate in art competitions, and much more.

If your school doesn't already have an art or photography club, start one yourself. Ask your art teachers to help you get started; most likely, they'll be overjoyed to find a group of kids who are willing and interested in exploring art or photography in more depth. They will probably be happy to assist, or at least steer you in the right direction. Like other school clubs or teams, an art or photography club needs the leadership of a teacher, especially if you're thinking of using school supplies and facilities.

Learn about Art Tools and Supplies

Paintbrushes, paint, ink, pencils, paper, clay, cutting knives, plaster of paris, beads, balsa wood, art-related computer software, cameras, developing equipment, and basic restoration materials. These are just some of the tools and supplies art professionals use to create their art. These items can be found at your school's art studio, local art supply stores, or through other methods. Some museums, such as the Tacoma Art Museum (http://www.tacomaartmuseum.org), even offer hands-on exhibits where you can examine tools used in the creation of art. Maybe your local museum offers a similar program. By experimenting with these items, you'll learn more about your interests in the field. For example, after trying out watercolors and oils, you might decide that you enjoy the longer creative process involved in working with oil paint. Or maybe throwing clay

or creating art on a computer is more your speed.

Compete in an Art Contest

Entering your work in an art contest or competition is an excellent way to see how your abilities match up with other artists. Schools, libraries, galleries, and art councils in nearly every town and city offer such opportunities to aspiring and experienced artists. Another good source is the National Endowment for the Arts, which offers information about competitions and other arts-related activities at the state level at its Web site, http://arts.endow.gov. Ask your art teacher to help you find art contests in your area or search the Web to find competitions near you. Visit the following Web sites to get started: FanArtReview.com (http://www.fanartreview.com), Art Wanted.com (http://www.artwanted.com), Art Deadlines List (http://artdeadlineslist.com).

Join an Association

Many professional art associations offer membership to high school and college students. Membership benefits may include the chance to participate in association-sponsored competitions, seminars, and conferences; subscriptions to magazines that provide the latest industry information (some of them geared specifically toward students); mentoring and networking opportunities, and chances to apply for financial aid. Read "Look to the Pros" in Section 4, "What Can I do Right Now?," for more information on associations that offer student membership.

Participate in a Summer Program

Many colleges and universities offer summer programs for highly motivated high school students who are interested in learning more about art and earning college credit in the process. These programs usually include workshops, seminars, gallery tours, exhibitions, and other activities that introduce you to art. You'll also get a chance to talk with art faculty and students (so have your list of questions about the field ready) and exhibit your art at program-sponsored exhibitions. These activities will allow you to meet other young people who are interested in the field and help you to learn more about art specialties. Summer programs are covered in depth in Section 4: What Can I Do Right Now: Get Involved: A Directory of Camps, Programs, Competitions, Etc. Visit the section for further information.

Land an Internship

It's never too soon to begin looking for hands-on experience in the art world, and an internship, either after school, on the weekends, or during the summer, is an easy way to get started. Although many more internships are available to college students, that shouldn't keep you from trying to find a local museum, gallery, company, or other arts-related employer who would be willing to exchange experience for a little extra help. Start with the obvious places. Ask your art teachers if they know of any museums, galleries, or companies in your area that offer internships or might be interested in having help with projects. Contact adults you, your parents, or teachers know who are art professionals. Where do they work? Could their company or workplace use your assistance? Be as enterprising as possible. If these leads don't pan out, move on to less obvious places. For example, look through the career chapters in this book. Brainstorm all of the different possibilities, and then ask your parents and friends for their ideas and suggestions.

Conduct an Information Interview or Job Shadow a Worker

Another way to learn about art careers is to conduct an information interview with or job shadow an art professional. What is an information interview? An information interview is simply a phone or in-person conversation with an art professional about his or her job. You can learn more about why they chose their specialty, their daily tasks, the tools and other equipment they use to do their job, what skills are required, and how best to prepare for the field. Remember to do the following when conducting an information interview: dress (if you are conducting the interview in person) and act appropriately, arrive or call on time, have written questions prepared, listen closely and don't interrupt the subject while he or she is talking, have a notepad and pen ready to record the subject's responses, don't overstay your welcome (if the subject has volunteered 20 minutes of his or her time, than stick to that time frame), and be sure to thank the subject both verbally and in writing (send a thank you via mail soon after the interview) for his or her time.

Job shadowing simply means observing someone at their job. In the case of art professionals, you might shadow them as they work in their studios, art conservation laboratories, galleries, museums, classrooms, auction houses, or health care settings. Remember to do the following when shadowing a worker: dress and act appropriately, arrive on time, take plenty of notes, be positive (if the job seems boring, don't say so!), follow the ground rules established by the subject, and thank the subject both verbally and in writing for the opportunity.

Ask your art teacher to help you arrange an information interview or job shadowing opportunity. Maybe one of your parents has an artist friend you could job shadow. You could also take the initiative and call or e-mail the public relations department of an art museum or gallery near you to see if they can refer you to an art professional. Some art associations may also offer these opportunities to student members.

Get a Job

Take your internship experiences to the next level and look for paid jobs that not only use your blossoming art experience, but also provide you with the opportunity to add to your existing knowledge. Challenge yourself. Start by contacting the same companies or organizations you used to search for internships. Now that you have some practical experience under your belt, they may be more inclined to offer you an internship or, better yet, a paying position.

Don't think small, but be realistic. As hard as it is to get internships as a high school student, it's even more difficult to get jobs. If you're finding that employers are saving those choice positions for college students, aim just a little bit lower. Let employers know how interested you are in learning from the ground up and you just might find yourself performing data entry or answering phones at an art gallery—and taking home a nice paycheck.

If you still turn up empty-handed, resort to the same tactics that helped you locate more unusual opportunities for internships. Brainstorm the specific tasks which different art professionals complete. Since many art professionals are self-employed, they often need to handle both the creative and the business-oriented tasks of running a business. An artist may not realize how much time he or she is spending on marketing, sales, and recordkeeping—valuable time that keeps him or her from what they really love: creating art. Perhaps you can take on some of these tasks to give the artist more time to paint or draw or photograph or do whatever they do. Maybe there's an art therapist in private practice near you who needs someone to answer phones and schedule appointments, or an art dealer who needs someone to run errands or prepare paintings for shipment. You might find you have to work for free for a probationary period until you learn the ropes, but in the end, you'll have a paying job that will give you valuable experience.

SECTION 4

What Can I Do Right Now?

Get Involved: A Directory of Camps, Programs, and Competitions

Now that you've read about some of the different careers available in the arts, you may be anxious to experience this field for yourself, to find out what it's really like. Or perhaps you already feel certain that this is the career path for you and want to get started on it right away. Whichever is the case, this section is for you! There are plenty of things you can do right now to learn about art careers while gaining valuable experience. Just as important, you'll get to meet new friends and see new places, too.

In the following pages you will find programs designed to pique your interest in the arts and start preparing you for a career. You already know that there are a wide variety of options available, and that to work in it you need a solid education and well-developed artistic skills (in many cases). Since the first step toward an arts career will be gaining that education, following are more than 35 programs that will start you on your way. Some are special introductory sessions, others are actual college courses—one of them may be right for you. Take time to read over the listings and see how each compares to your situation: how committed you are to the arts, how much of your money and free time you're willing to devote to it, and how the program will help you after high school. These listings are divided

into categories, with the type of program printed right after its name or the name of the sponsoring organization.

❏ THE CATEGORIES

Camps

When you see an activity that is classified as a camp, don't automatically start packing your tent and mosquito repellent. Where academic study is involved, the term "camp" often simply means a residential program including both educational and recreational activities. It's sometimes hard to differentiate between such camps and other study programs, but if the sponsoring organization calls it a camp, so do we! For an extended list of arts-related camps, visit http://www.kidscamps.com/art/art.html.

College Courses/Summer Study

These terms are linked because most college courses offered to students your age must take place in the summer, when you are out of school. At the same time, many summer study programs are sponsored by colleges and universities that want to attract future students and give them a head start in higher education. Summer study of almost any type is a good idea because it keeps your mind and your study skills sharp over the long vacation. Summer study at a college offers any number of additional benefits, including giving you the tools to make a well-informed decision about your future academic career.

Competitions

Competitions are fairly self-explanatory, but you should know that there are only a few in this book for the following reason: many art competitions are at the local and regional levels and are impractical to list here. What this means, however, is that if you are interested in entering a competition, you shouldn't have much trouble finding one yourself. Your guidance counselor or art teacher can help you start searching in your area.

Conferences

Conferences for high school students are usually difficult to track down because most are for professionals in the field who gather to share new information and ideas with each other. Don't be discouraged, though. A number of professional organizations with student branches invite those student members to their conferences and plan special events for them. Some student branches even run their own conferences; check the directory of student organizations at the end of this section for possible leads. Even though there are no specific conferences listed in this book, they focus on some of the most current information available and also give you the chance to meet professionals who can answer your questions and even offer advice. Thus, be sure to investigate this option further.

Employment and Internship Opportunities

As you may already know from experience, employment opportunities for teenagers can be very limited. Even internships are most often reserved for college students who have completed at least one or two years of study in the field. Still, if you're very determined to find an internship or paid position in the arts, there may be ways to find one. See Section 3: "Do It Yourself" in this book for some suggestions.

Field Experience

This is something of a catch-all category for activities that don't exactly fit the other descriptions. But anything called a field experience in this book is always a good opportunity to get out and explore the work of art professionals.

Membership

When an organization is in this category, it simply means that you are welcome to pay your dues and become a card-carrying member. Formally joining any organization brings the benefits of meeting others who share your interests, finding opportunities to get involved, and keeping up with current events. Depending on how active you are, the contacts you make and the experiences you gain may help when the time comes to apply to colleges or look for a job.

In some organizations, you pay a special student rate and receive benefits similar to regular members. Many organizations, however, are now starting student branches with their own benefits and publications. As in any field, make sure you understand exactly what the benefits of membership are before you join.

Finally, don't let membership dues discourage you from making contact with these organizations. Some charge dues as low as $25 because they know that students are perpetually short of funds. When the annual dues are higher, think of the money as an investment in your future and then consider if it is too much to pay.

❑ PROGRAM DESCRIPTIONS

Once you've started to look at the individual listings themselves, you'll find that they contain a lot of information. Naturally, there is a general description of each program, but wherever possible we also have included the following details.

Application Information

Each listing notes how far in advance you'll need to apply for the program or position, but the simple rule is to apply as far in advance as possible. This ensures that you won't miss out on a great opportunity simply because other people applied before you. It also means that you will get a timely decision on your application, so if you are not accepted, you'll still have some time to apply elsewhere. As for the things that make up your application—essays, recommendations, portfolios, and so forth—we've tried to tell you what's involved, but be sure to contact the program about specific requirements before you submit anything.

Background Information

This includes such information as the date the program was established, the name of the organization that is sponsoring it financially, and the faculty and staff who will be there for you. This can help you—and your family—gauge the quality and reliability of the program.

Classes and Activities

Classes and activities change from year to year, depending on popularity, availability of instructors, and many other factors. Nevertheless, colleges and universities quite consistently offer the same or similar classes, even in their summer sessions. Courses like "Introduction to Painting" and "Drawing 101," for example, are simply indispensable. So you can look through the listings and see which programs offer foundational courses like these and which offer courses on more variable topics. As for activities, we note when you have access to recreational facilities on campus, and it's usually a given that special social and cultural activities will be arranged for most programs.

Contact Information

Wherever possible, we have given the title of the person whom you should contact instead of the name because people change jobs so frequently. If no title is given and you are calling an organization, simply tell the person who answers the phone the name of the program that interests you and he or she will forward your call. If you are writing, include the line "Attention: Summer Study Program" (or whatever is appropriate after "Attention") somewhere on the envelope. This will help to ensure that your letter goes to the person in charge of that program.

Credit

Where academic programs are concerned, we sometimes note that high school or college credit is available to those who have completed them. This means that the program can count toward your high school diploma or a future college degree just like a regular course. Obviously, this can be very useful, but it's important to note that rules about accepting such credit vary from school to school. Before you commit to a program offering high school credit, check with your guidance counselor to see if it is acceptable to your school. As for programs offering college credit, check with your chosen college (if you have one) to see if they will accept it.

Eligibility and Qualifications

The main eligibility requirement to be concerned about is age or grade in school. A term frequently used in relation to grade level is "rising," as in "rising senior": someone who will be a senior when the next school year begins. This is especially important where summer programs are concerned. A number of university-based programs make admissions decisions partly in consideration of GPA, class rank, and standardized test scores. This is mentioned in the listings, but you must contact the program for specific numbers. If you are worried that your GPA or your ACT scores, for example, aren't good enough, don't let them stop you from applying to programs that consider such things in the admissions process. Often, a fine essay, an attractive portfolio, or even an example of your dedication and eagerness can compensate for statistical weaknesses.

Facilities

We tell you where you'll be living, studying, eating, and having fun during these programs, but there isn't enough room to go into all the details. Some of those details can be important: what is and isn't accessible for people with disabilities, whether the site of a summer program has air-conditioning, and how modern the laboratory and computer equipment are. You can expect most program brochures and application materials to address these concerns, but if you still have questions about the facilities, just call the program's administration and ask.

Financial Details

While a few of the programs listed here are fully underwritten by collegiate and corporate sponsors, most of them rely on you for at least some of their funding. Prices and fees for 2004–05 are given here, but you should bear in mind that costs rise slightly almost every year. You and your parents must take costs into consideration when choosing a program. Financial aid is noted wherever it is available, but most programs will do their best to ensure that a shortage of funds does not prevent you from taking part.

Residential Versus Commuter Options

Simply put, some programs prefer that participating students live with other participants and staff members, others do not, and still others leave the decision entirely to the students. As a rule, residential programs are suitable for young people who live out of town or even out of state, as well as for local residents. They generally provide a better overview of college life than programs in which you're only on campus for a few hours a day, and they're a way to test how well you cope with living away from home. Commuter programs may be viable only if you live near the program site or if you can stay with relatives who do. Bear in mind that for residential programs especially, the travel between your home and the location of the activity is almost always your responsibility and can significantly increase the cost of participation.

Finally . . .

Ultimately, there are three important things to bear in mind concerning all of the programs listed in this volume. The first is that things change. Staff members come and go, funding is added or withdrawn, and supply and demand determine which programs continue and which terminate. Dates, times, and costs vary widely because of a number of factors. Because of this, the information presented here, although it is as current and detailed as possible, is not enough to help you reach your final decision. If you are interested in a program, you must write, call, fax, or e-mail the organization concerned to get the latest and most complete information available. This has the added benefit of putting you in touch with someone who can deal with your individual questions and problems.

Another important point to keep in mind when considering these programs is that the people who run them provided the information printed here. The editors of this book haven't attended the programs and don't endorse them: you are simply given the information with which to begin your own research. You are the only one who can decide which programs are right for you.

The final thing to bear in mind is that the programs listed here are just the tip of the iceberg. No book can possibly cover all of the opportunities that are available to you—partly because they are so numerous and are constantly coming and going, but also because some are waiting to be discovered. For instance, you may be very interested in taking a college course but don't see the college that interests you in the listings. Call their admissions office! Even if they don't have a special program for high school students, they might be able to make some kind of arrangements for you to visit or sit in on a class. Use the ideas behind these listings and take the initiative to turn them into opportunities.

❏ THE PROGRAMS
Academic Study Associates
College Courses/Summer Study

Academic Study Associates has been offering residential and commuter pre-college summer programs for young people for more than 20 years. It offers college credit classes and enrichment opportunities in a variety of academic fields, including the arts, at the University of Massachusetts–

Amherst, the University of California–Berkeley, Emory University, and Oxford University. In addition to classroom/studio work, students participate in field trips, mini-clinics, and extracurricular activities. Programs are usually three to four weeks in length. Fees and deadlines vary for these programs—visit the ASA Web site for further details. Options are also available for middle school students.

Academic Study Associates (ASA)

ASA Programs
10 New King Street
White Plains, NY 10604
800-752-2250
summer@asaprograms.com
http://www.asaprograms.com/home/asa_home.asp

After School at the Museum Program at the Los Angeles County Museum of Art

Field Experience

Students in grades three through twelve can participate in the After School at the Museum Program at the Los Angeles County Museum of Art. The program introduces students to the museum's collections one afternoon per week for eight weeks. Students learn how to observe art and participate in gallery activities and art workshops. For more information, have your teacher or principal contact

Los Angeles County Museum of Art

After School at the Museum Program Coordinator
Education Department

5905 Wilshire Boulevard
Los Angeles, CA 90036
http://www.lacma.org

American Council for International Studies' Summer Fast Track and Summer Adventure Programs

College Courses/Summer Study

The American Council for International Studies (ACIS) offers two study abroad programs for high school students who are interested in art and other subjects. Students in its Summer Fast Track Program can take college courses for credit in England, France, Italy, Spain, and Russia. If you don't want to leave the United States, there is also a program available in California. Typical classes vary by country, but past classes included Introduction to Photography, Introduction to the Museums and Galleries of London, Aspects of French Fashion and Design, Introduction to High Renaissance Art, History of Russian Art, Visual Arts: Drawing and Painting, and various language immersion courses. Fees, the number of college credits available, and courses vary by program; visit the ACIS Web site for further details. The council also offers less structured educational programs in Europe, Costa Rica, Italy, Australia, and New Zealand via its Summer Adventure Program. Programs last from 17 to 30 days. Students are immersed in the artistic and cultural history of their host countries, stay in three- to four-star hotels, and are provided with breakfast and dinner daily. Contact the council for more information. Scholarships are available for both programs.

American Council for International Studies

c/o American Institute for Foreign
  Study
Summer Programs
River Plaza
9 West Broad Street
Stamford, CT 06902-3788
877-795-0813
accounts@acis.com
http://www.summeradvantage.com

Artists' Woods Tweens 'n Teen Art Intensives

Camps

Artists' Woods offers summer art classes to students from ages three to 18 years old. A wide variety of art classes are available, including Digital Photography, Acrylic Painting, Figurative Sculpture, Graphic Design, Watercolor Painting, Art of Woodworking, Oil Painting, Figure Drawing, and Art Essentials. Classes are held from late June through early September. Visit the camp's Web site for information on fees and class dates.

Artists' Woods

403 Abrahams Path, Box 594
Amagansett, NY 11930
631-267-7910
TNT@arttistswoods.com
http://www.artistswoods.com

The Arts! at Maryland

College Courses/Summer Study

The Arts! at Maryland Program is sponsored by the University of Maryland for motivated high school juniors and seniors who are interested in visual arts, creative writing, music, theatre arts, and dance. Participants in the three-week program spend July exploring the field of visual arts and taking a college-level course—either Drawing I or Computer Graphics. Students will spend time in the studio, the classroom, and on field trips to art galleries and studios. College credit is awarded to students who satisfactorily complete the course. Participants can commute or live in the residence halls at the University of Maryland and take their meals on campus or in selected College Park restaurants. To apply, you must submit an application form, an essay, two letters of recommendation, a current transcript, and an application fee by mid-May. Admissions decisions are based primarily on the recommendations, a GPA of 3.0 or better, and overall academic ability. For further details (including information on cost of tuition) and an application form, visit the Web site listed below or contact the Summer Sessions and Special Programs staff.

Summer Sessions and Special Programs

Mitchell Building, 1st Floor
University of Maryland
College Park, MD 20742
877-989-7762
http://www.summer.umd.edu/c/
admissions/courses/taam

Boston University High School Honors Program/Summer Challenge Program

College Courses/Summer Study

Two summer educational opportunities are available for high school students interested in art and other majors. Rising high school seniors can participate in the High School Honors Program, which offers six-week, for-credit undergraduate study at the university. Students take two for-credit classes (up to eight credits) alongside regular Boston University students, live in dorms on campus, and participate in extracurricular activities and tours of local attractions. The program typically begins in early July. Students who demonstrate financial need may be eligible for financial aid. Tuition for the program is approximately $3,550, with registration/program fees ($350) and room and board options ($1,598 to $1,718) extra. Rising high school sophomores, juniors, and seniors in the university's Summer Challenge Program learn about college life and take college classes in a noncredit setting. The program lasts two weeks and is offered in three sessions. Students get to choose two seminars (which feature lectures, group and individual work, project-based assignments, and field trips) from a total of eight available programs. Seminar choices include visual arts, business, law, international politics, creative writing, persuasive writing, psychology, and science. Students live in dorms on campus and participate in extracurricular activities and tours of local attractions. The cost of the program is approximately $2,550 (which includes tuition, a room charge, meals, and sponsored activities). Visit the university's Summer Programs Web site for more information.

Boston University Summer Programs
755 Commonwealth Avenue
Boston, MA 02215
617-353-5124
summer@bu.edu
http://www.bu.edu/summer/highschool

Camp Ballibay
Camp

Camp Ballibay, established in 1964, is accredited by the American Camping Association. It offers programs (two to nine weeks in length) for students ages 6 to 16 in visual arts, photography, theater, vocal and instrumental music, ballet, modern jazz and tap dance, video, radio, and technical theater. The visual arts program offers the following specialties: drawing, painting, ceramics, photography, printmaking, and other media. In addition to classes, students participate in art exhibitions and various extracurricular activities. Campers stay in cabins and have access to art studios, theater buildings, a swimming pool, a riding area, tennis courts, sports fields, an infirmary, a camp store, and a dining hall. Tuition for this residential camp ranges from $1,775 to $5,775 depending on the length of the program. Contact the camp for further information.

Camp Ballibay
One Ballibay Road
Camptown, PA 18815
570-746-3223
jannone@ballibay.com
http://www.ballibay.com

Challenge Program at St. Vincent College

College Courses/Summer Study

The Challenge Program, offered by St. Vincent College, gives gifted, creative, and talented students in ninth through twelfth grades the opportunity to explore new and stimulating subjects that most high schools just can't cover. If you qualify for this program and are highly motivated, you can spend one week in July on the campus of St. Vincent College taking courses such as Caricatures in Clay, The Creative Mind, and Designs in Architecture. Should you choose, you may live on campus, meeting and socializing with other students who share your ambitions and interests. Resident students pay a total of about $600 for the week while commuters pay closer to $500. A limited amount of financial aid is available. For more information about Challenge and details of this year's course offerings, contact the program coordinator. There is a similar Challenge program for students in the sixth through ninth grades, usually held one week before the high school session.

Challenge Program at St. Vincent College
c/o Program Coordinator
300 Fraser Purchase Road
Latrobe, PA 15650
412-532-5093
info@stvincent.edu
http://www.stvincent.edu/challenge_home

College and Careers Program

College Courses/Summer Study

The Rochester Institute of Technology (RIT) offers its College and Careers Program for rising seniors who want to experience college life and explore career options in art, design, crafts, and other subject areas. The program, founded in 1990, enables students to spend a Friday and Saturday on campus, living in the dorms and attending four sessions on the career areas of their choice. Past arts-related sections included Work with Glass, Woodworking and Furniture Design; Ceramics: Hands on Clay; Graphic Design: Creativity, Composition, and Computers; New Media Design and Imaging; Printmaking; Illustration; Medical Illustration; Painting; and Photography: Basic In-Camera Special Effects. In each session, participants work with RIT students and faculty to gain hands-on experience in the subject area. This residential program is held twice each summer, usually once in mid-July and again in early August. The registration deadline is one week before the start of the program, but space is limited and students are accepted on a first come, first served basis. For further information about the program and specific sessions on offer, contact the RIT admissions office.

College and Careers Program
Rochester Institute of Technology
Office of Admissions
60 Lomb Memorial Drive
Rochester, NY 14623-5604
585-475-6631
https://ambassador.rit.edu/careers2006/

Cornell University Summer College
College Courses/Summer Study

As part of its Summer College for High School Students, Cornell University offers an Exploration in Art seminar for students who have completed their junior or senior years. The Summer College session runs for six weeks from late June until early August. It is largely a residential program designed to acquaint you with all aspects of college life. The Exploration in Art seminar is one of several such seminars Cornell offers to allow students to survey various disciplines within the field and speak with working professionals. The seminar meets several times per week and includes lectures and field trips to art galleries and artists' studios. In addition, Summer College participants take two college-level courses of their own choosing from a total of 60 courses offered. The university suggests that students take at least one of the following classes: Introductory Painting, Introductory Sculpture, Life and Still-Life Drawing, Electronic Imaging in Art, and Survey of European Art: Renaissance to Modern. You must bear in mind that these are regular undergraduate courses condensed into a very short time span, so they are especially challenging and demanding. Besides the course material, you will learn time-management and study skills to prepare you for a program of undergraduate study.

Cornell University awards letter grades and full undergraduate credit for the two courses you complete, but none for the Exploration. Residents live and eat on campus, and enjoy access to the university's recreational facilities, the Herbert F. Johnson Museum of Art, and special activities. Academic fees total around $3,400, while housing, food, and recreation fees amount to an additional $1,600. Books, travel, and an application fee are extra. A very limited amount of financial aid is available. Applications are due in early May, although Cornell advises that you submit them well in advance of the deadline; those applying for financial aid must submit their applications by early April. Further information and details of the application procedure are available from the Summer College office.

Cornell University Summer College for High School Students
Summer College
B20 Day Hall
Ithaca, NY 14853-2801
607-255-6203
http://www.sce.cornell.edu/sc/explorations/art.php

Dickinson College Pre-College Summer Programs
College Courses/Summer Study

Rising high school juniors and seniors who are interested in exploring art and other fields may want to participate in Pre-College Summer Programs at Dickinson College. The month-long program, available in both residential and commuter options, exposes young people to college-level classes in their field of interest. Recent arts-related courses included Introduction to Photography and Introduction to Digital Photography. The residential program costs approximately $5,000, which includes accommodations in Dickinson College dormitories, a full meal plan, special events, and field trips. Additional fees for spending money and books are required. Contact the director of Summer Programs for information on the costs of commuter options. Some financial aid is available.

Dickinson College

Summer Programs
c/o Director of Summer Programs
PO Box 1773
Carlisle, PA 17013
717-254-8782
summer@dickinson.edu
http://www.dickinson.edu/summer/precollege.html

Early Experience Program
College Courses/Summer Study

The University of Denver invites academically gifted high school students interested in art and other subjects to apply for its Early Experience Program, which involves participating in university-level classes during the school year and especially during the summer. This is a commuter-only program. Interested students must submit a completed application (with essay), official high school transcript, standardized test results (PACT/ACT/PSAT/SAT), a letter of recommendation from a counselor or teacher, and have a minimum GPA of 3.0. Contact the Early Experience Program Coordinator for more information, including application forms, available classes, and current fees.

University of Denver

Office of Academic Youth Programs
Early Experience Program
1981 South University Boulevard
Denver, CO 80208
303-871-2663
http://www.du.edu/education/ces/ee.html

Exploration Summer Programs
College Courses/Summer Study

Exploration Summer Programs (ESP) has been offering academic summer enrichment programs to students for nearly 30 years. Rising high school sophomores, juniors, and seniors can participate in ESP's Senior Program at Yale University. Two three-week residential and day sessions are available and are typically held in June and July. Participants can choose from more than 80 courses in the visual arts and other areas of study. Students entering the 11th or 12th grades can take college seminars, which provide coursework that is similar to that of first-year college study. All courses and seminars are ungraded and not-for-credit. In addition to academics, students participate in extracurricular activities such as tours, sports, concerts, weekend recreational trips, college trips, and discussions of current events and other issues. Tuition for the Residential Senior Program is approximately $4,100 for one session and $7,400 for two sessions. Day session tuition ranges from approximately $2,100 for one session to $3,795 for two sessions. A limited number of need-based partial and full scholarships are available. Programs are also available for students in grades four through nine. Contact ESP for more information.

Exploration Summer Programs
470 Washington Street
PO Box 368
Norwood, MA 02062
781-762-7400
http://www.explo.org

FanArtReview.com
Competitions
FanArtReview.com is an online community of photographers and artists. It offers a variety of eclectic contests for artists and photographers of all skill levels. Visit the Web site for more information.

FanArtReview.com
http://www.fanartreview.com

High School Internship Program at The Museum of Modern Art
Employment and Internship Opportunities
Students from New York City public high schools who are interested in art are eligible to participate in the Museum of Modern Art's High School Internship Program. The program runs from February through May (students must work at least two afternoons a week), but many interns go on to participate in the Museum's Summer Program (June through August, up to five days a week) for an hourly stipend. To apply, students should submit a resume, a cover letter that details their interest in the program, and a letter of recommendation from a teacher, counselor, or school administra-tor. Contact the High School Internship coordinator for more information or visit the museum's Web site.

The Museum of Modern Art
Attn: High School Internship Coordinator
11 West 53rd Street
New York, NY 10019
http://www.moma.org/education/
internships_high.html

High School Summer Institute at Columbia College Chicago
College Courses/Summer Study
Rising high school sophomores, juniors, and seniors can take courses in one of 18 academic areas (including art and design and photography) for college credit via Columbia's five-week High School Summer Institute. Recent arts-related classes included Introduction to Graphic Design, Fundamentals of Fashion Design, Product Design, Fine Art Mixed Media, Computers for Art, Introduction to Photography, and Digital Photography. Students stay in residence halls on campus; the approximately $1,400 room and board fee includes housing, an evening meal each day, and evening and weekend activities. Tuition is $150 per credit hour; there may be an additional charge for books and other materials. A limited number of scholarships are available. Contact the Institute for further details.

Columbia College Chicago
High School Summer Institute
600 South Michigan Avenue
Chicago, IL 60605

312-344-7130
summerinstitute@colum.edu
http://www.colum.edu/admissions/
hs_institute

Hila Science Camp

Camps

Hila Science Camp offers both residential and day camps in the Ottawa Valley, close to Beachburg, Ontario. Hila, established in 1984, features a variety of programs with an emphasis on science and technology (but also includes a program on digital photography and video). Participants in the digital photography program will learn how to use digital cameras, create artwork on computers using Corel-Draw and PhotoPaint, and transfer their artwork onto T-shirts and posters. In addition to their major program, participants can collect specimens, go on archaeological digs, hunt for fossils, and gaze at the stars through Hila's eight-foot reflecting telescope. Residential camp lasts one week, from Sunday afternoon through the following Friday. Campers sleep in large dome-style tents, and Hila facilities include a dining hall, basketball court, darkroom, electronics shop, computer room, and a flying field. Day camp runs Monday through Friday, 9:00 A.M. to 5:00 P.M. Hila offers seven camp sessions, beginning in late June, and all programs are offered in all sessions. A week of day camp at Hila costs about $335; contact Hila for current prices for residential camp. Kits and equipment for various programs cost extra. Each program enrolls a maximum of 34 students on a first-come, first-served basis. If you live in the Ottawa Valley, some scholarships are available. Hila is happy to provide you with more details on all matters.

Hila Science Camp
382 Hila Road
RR #2
Pembroke, ON Canada K8A 6W3
613-582-3632
hila@hilaroad.com
http://www.hilaroad.com

Idyllwild Arts Academy Summer Program

Camps

Since 1950, the Idyllwild Arts Academy has been offering students intensive opportunities to explore the arts. The Academy's Youth Arts Center offers a variety of art programs for students between ages 13 and 18, including art exploration, black and white photography, youth ceramics, photo explorations, world art tour, youth jewelry workshop, computer animation, video production studio, drawing and painting, and portfolio preparation. Commuter and resident options are available. Most sessions last two weeks, but the drawing and painting program consists of three two-week sessions. Contact the program for information on tuition and fees for room and board. Scholarships are available and are awarded on the basis of financial need and the artistic ability of the applicant.

**Idyllwild Arts Academy
    Summer Program**
52500 Temecula Drive, PO Box 38
Idyllwild, CA 92549-0038

951-659-2171, ext. 2223
http://www.idyllwildarts.org

Interlochen Arts Camp
Camps

Interlochen, located near scenic Traverse City, Michigan, is one of the premier art camps in the United States for young visual artists, musicians, dancers, actors, and writers. High school students who are interested in the visual arts can participate in the following three- or six-week programs: advanced drawing, advanced painting, ceramics, drawing, digital image, fibers, metals, painting, photography, printmaking and graphics, and sculpture. They can also participate in more than 50 installations, exhibitions, and performance works on campus. Students stay in cabins with 10 to 18 other students and counselors and have access to a private beach, tennis courts, division headquarters, and laundry (students are required to do their own laundry). Extracurricular activities include concerts by well-known musicians, dances, viewing gallery exhibits, arts and crafts, sports, and outdoor activities. The tuition for this camp varies ($3,300 or $5,540 or $5,582) by program, but includes classes, room and board, group instruction, required private lessons, use of all recreational facilities, and admission to student and faculty performances. Financial aid is available based on the financial need and the artistic ability of the applicant. Programs are also available for students in grades three through eight. Applications for all programs are due in February. Contact the camp for more information.

Interlochen Arts Camp
Admissions Office
PO Box 199
Interlochen, MI 49643
231-276-7472
admissions@interlochen.org
http://www.interlochen.org/camp/
summer_camp_programs/visual_arts

Intern Exchange International, Ltd.
Employment and Internship Opportunities

High school students ages 16 to 18 (including graduating seniors) who are interested in gaining real-life experience in art can participate in a month-long summer internship in London, England. Participants will work as interns at one of London's most prestigious art galleries, researching paintings, cataloging art, helping to negotiate art sales, and visiting the studios of participating artists. Other interns will be assigned to auction houses, such as Sotheby's, and help professionals prepare for an auction. The cost of the program is approximately $6,200 plus airfare; this fee includes tuition, housing (students live in residence halls at the University of London), breakfast and dinner daily, housekeeping service, linens and towels, special dinner events, weekend trips and excursions, group activities including scheduled theatre, and a Tube Pass. Contact Intern Exchange International for more information.

Intern Exchange International, Ltd.
2606 Bridgewood Circle
Boca Raton, FL 33434-4118
561-477-2434

info@internexchange.com
http://www.internexchange.com

Long Lake Camp for the Arts
Camps

Long Lake Camp for the Arts offers a variety of arts-based programs to young people ages 10 through 16. Programs include fine arts, theatre, dance, music, circus, and video/film. The fine arts program offers the following studios which are taught by approximately 25 artists-in-residence: batik and tie-dye, cartooning, ceramics, computer graphics and animation, design and sewing, drawing, environmental art, jewelry, mixed media, painting, photography, printing, printmaking, sculpture, silk-screen fabric design, silversmithing, and weaving. In addition to program-related activities, campers can participate in sports and outdoor recreational outings. Three- and six-week sessions are available and cost $4,450 and $7,950 respectively. Tuition includes food and lodging, private lessons, craft materials, and all programs of instruction except horseback riding. Contact the camp for more information.

Long Lake Camp for the Arts
199 Washington Avenue
Dobbs Ferry, NY 10522
marc@longlakecamp.com
http://www.longlakecamp.com

Marie Walsh Sharpe Art Foundation Summer Seminar
Camps/Summer Study

The Marie Walsh Sharpe Art Foundation Summer Seminar is a program that helps artistically gifted high school juniors develop their skills and understanding in the visual arts via college-level classes. The seminar is a scholarship program that offers full tuition, room and board, and all seminar related expenses, excluding transportation. It is held on the campus of Colorado College in Colorado Springs, Colorado. Three two-week seminars are available each summer—typically in June and July. Students receive instruction from artists-in-residence. Topics covered include technical skills, careers in art, and developing a portfolio. Students will also tour local museums and paint and draw in the scenic mountains near the college. Participants stay in dormitories, eat in the campus dining hall, and have access to all campus facilities. Applicants must submit an application form, six to 10 slides of their original work (the seminar emphasizes drawing and painting), a written personal statement expressing their most memorable life experience, and a recommendation from an art teacher. Applications are due in April. An average of 21 students are selected per session. Contact the program officer for more information.

Marie Walsh Sharpe Art Foundation
c/o Kimberly Taylor, Program Officer
830 North Tejon Street, Suite 120
Colorado Springs, CO 80903
719-635-3220
sharpeartfdn@qwest.net
http://www.sharpeartfdn.org/summer1.htm

National Council on Education for the Ceramic Arts

Membership

Students of all ages can become members of the National Council on Education for the Ceramic Arts. Membership benefits include a copy of the Council's annual Membership Directory and subscriptions to the NCECA *Journal* and NCECA News.

> ### National Council on Education for the Ceramic Arts
> 77 Erie Village Square, Suite 280
> Erie, CO 80516-6996
> 866-266-2322
> office@nceca.net
> http://www.nceca.net

National Sculpture Society (NSS)

Membership

The NSS is the oldest organization of professional sculptors in the United States. Creators and lovers of sculpture can apply to become Associate Members of the organization. Members receive subscriptions to *Sculpture Review* and the *NSS News Bulletin,* prospectuses for exhibitions sponsored by the Society, and invitations to NSS programs.

> ### National Sculpture Society
> 237 Park Avenue
> New York, NY 10017
> 212-764-5645
> http://www.sculpturereview.com/nss.html

Open Art Studio at the Tacoma Art Museum

Field Experience

Visitors to the Tacoma Art Museum in Tacoma, Washington, can get hands-on experience with art by visiting its Open Art Studio. You can study art toolkits on the studio's walls that show how the works currently being exhibited were created. Additionally, tables with briefcases contain items and tools that will help visitors learn about a wide range of art techniques such as sketching and watercolor. Volunteer opportunities are also available at the museum.

> ### Tacoma Art Museum
> 1701 Pacific Avenue
> Tacoma, WA 98402
> 253-272-4258
> info@tacomaartmuseum.org
> http://www.tacomaartmuseum.org

Oxbow Summer Art Camp

Camps

High school students ages 14 through 16 are eligible to apply for admission to the Oxbow Summer Art Camp, which is located in picturesque Napa Valley, California. The two-and-a-half-week program (which is available in both commuter and residential options) immerses young people in drawing, painting, sculpture, digital art, and photography. Facilities include dormitories, art studios, a dining hall, and an organic garden. Only 36 boarding campers and 26 commuter students are chosen for each session. Tuition for boarding students is approximately $2,880, while commuter students pay about $3,000 (which includes three meals a day). Visit Oxbow's Web site for a virtual tour and more information.

Oxbow Summer Art Camp
530 Third Street
Napa, CA 94559
707-255-6000
summercamp@oxbowschool.org
http://www.oxbowschool.org/
summercamp

Summer Acceleration Program in Art at Skidmore College
College Courses/Summer Study

High school sophomores, juniors, and seniors who are interested in studio art can apply for enrollment in Skidmore's Summer Acceleration Program in Art. During the month-long program, students are required to enroll in two courses—available in credit and noncredit formats. Courses include Introduction to Painting, Basic Ceramics, Visual Concepts, Emphasis on Life Drawing, Form and Space, Color, Watercolor (Water Based Painting), Introduction to Fiber Arts, and Accelerated Programs in various art disciplines. Students live in dorms on campus, take courses with Skidmore students, and attend Advanced Placement (AP) workshops and lectures by visiting artists and art historians. Fees for the program are as follows: application fee, $30; room and board, $1,550; activity fee, $220; credit tuition, $1,305 (three credits) or $1,610 (four credits); and noncredit tuition per AP workshop, $850. Students may apply for scholarships on the basis of financial need and artistic merit. Applicants must submit a personal statement of interest in art and the program, a letter of recommendation from an art teacher, a high school transcript, and 8 to 10 color slides of their most recent work. Students who are applying for financial aid will need to submit additional documentation. For more information, visit the program's Web site.

Summer Acceleration Program in Art at Skidmore College
Program Coordinator
815 North Broadway
Saratoga Springs, NY 12866
http://www.skidmore.edu/academics/
art/summersix/accelerated_program

Summer Art Studio at the University of Wisconsin-Green Bay
Camps

Students entering grades 10 through 12 may participate in the University of Wisconsin-Green Bay's Summer Art Studio, a five-day arts immersion camp that is offered with both commuter and residential options. Recent courses included Acrylic Painting: From the Ordinary to the Extraordinary; Ceramics: Using The Potter's Wheel and Advanced Hand Building Techniques for Raku Firing; Computer Animation; Figure Drawing: Portrait Painting; Metals and Jewelry; Raw Metals and Ready-Mades; Advanced Photography: Using the Darkroom; Screen-Printing; Street Chic Shek: Creating Your Personal Style in Streetwear; and Experimental Watercolor. The fee for commuters is $185. The resident fee is $429, which includes instruction, room and board (participants are encouraged to bring a fan because there is no air-conditioning in the dorms), supervision by counselors, and evening activity transportation (there is an extra cost for evening activities). Some scholarships are available. The university also offers a Studio Art Program for middle school students. Contact the Office of Outreach and Extension for further information on both programs.

University of Wisconsin-Green Bay

Youth Opportunities Summer
   Camps
Office of Outreach and Extension
2420 Nicolet Drive
Green Bay, WI 54311-7001
800-892-2118
summercamps@uwgb.edu
http://www.uwgb.edu/camps

Summer College for High School Students at Syracuse University
College Courses/Summer Study

The Syracuse University Summer College for High School Students features two arts-related programs for those who have just completed their sophomore, junior, or senior year: art and design and fashion and textile design. The Summer College lasts six weeks and offers a residential option so participants can experience campus life while still in high school. Each arts-based program has several aims: to introduce you to the many specialties within the art or design profession; to help you match your aptitudes with possible careers; and to prepare you for college, both academically and socially. Students work in the studio, listen to lectures, take field trips to art galleries and other interesting places, and take part in a final exhibition of their work. All students are required to take two courses during the program and they receive college credit if they successfully complete the courses. Admission is competitive and is based on recommendations, test scores, and transcripts. The total cost of the residential program is about $5,300; the commuter option costs about $3,800. Some scholarships are available. The application deadline is in mid-May, or mid-April for those seeking financial aid. For further information, contact the Summer College.

Syracuse University Summer College for High School Students

111 Waverly Avenue, Suite 240
Syracuse, NY 13244-2320
315-443-5297
sumcoll@syr.edu
http://summercollege.syr.edu

Summer Program for Secondary School Program at Harvard University
College Courses/Summer Study

High school students who have completed their sophomore, junior, or senior years may apply to Harvard's Summer Program for Secondary School Program. Students who live on campus take either two four-unit courses or one eight-unit course for college credit. Commuting students may take only one four-unit course for college credit. Recent arts-related courses included Introduction to Still Photography, Principles of Graphic Design, Crucial Issues in Landscape Creation and Perception, and History of Western Art: Renaissance to the Present. In addition to academics, students can participate in extracurricular activities such as intramural sports, a trivia bowl, a talent show, and dances. Tuition for the program ranges from $2,125 (per four-unit course) to $4,250 (per eight-unit course). A non-refundable registration fee ($50), health insurance ($110), and room and board ($3,725) are extra. The application deadline for this program is mid-June. Contact the program for more information.

Harvard University
Summer Program for Secondary
   School Program
51 Brattle Street
Cambridge, MA 02138
617-495-4024
http://www.summer.harvard.edu

Summer Study at Penn State
College Courses/Summer Study

High school students who are interested in art or other fields can apply to participate in Penn State's Summer Study programs. The six-and-a-half-week College Credit Program begins in late June and offers the following arts-related classes: The Visual Arts and the Studio, Introduction to Drawing, Introduction to Painting, Introduction to Ceramics, and Renaissance to Modern Art. Students typically choose one college credit course (for three or four credits) and either an enrich-

ment class/workshop or the Kaplan SAT prep class. Students who have completed grades 10, 11, or 12 are eligible to apply. The three-and-a-half-week Non-Credit Enrichment Program is held in early July and features arts-related classes such as Channel Your Inner Chanel: Fashion and Design, A Course of a Different Color: Intro to Art, and Say Cheese!: Photography. Students who have completed the grades 9, 10, or 11 are eligible for the program. Tuition for the College Credit Program is approximately $6,000, while tuition for the Non-Credit Enrichment Program is approximately $4,000. Limited financial aid is available. Contact the program for more information.

Penn State University
Summer Study Program
University Park, PA 16804
800-666-2556
info@summerstudy.com
http://www.summerstudy.com/
pennstate

Summer Youth Programs
College Courses/Summer Study

Michigan Technological University (MTU) offers the Summer Youth Program for students in grades 6 through 11. Participants attend one of four weeklong sessions usually held during the months of July or August, choosing either to commute or to live on campus. Students explore one of many career fields—including art—through field trips and discussions with MTU faculty and other professionals. Classes offered typically include A Keweenaw Sculpture

Experience; Ceramics: Raku; Creative Arts; Drawing: The Universal Language; Graphic Design; Painting; Photography; and Sketching. The cost of the Summer Youth Program is $510 for the residential option, $300 for commuters. Applications are accepted up to one week before the program begins.

Summer Youth Program

Michigan Technological University
Youth Programs Office, Alumni
  House
1400 Townsend Drive
Houghton, MI 49931-1295
906-487-2219
http://youthprograms.mtu.edu

Talented and Gifted Program/ College Experience Program at Southern Methodist University

College Courses/Summer Study

Students in grades 8 through 10 can participate in Southern Methodist University's (SMU's) Talented and Gifted Program. The two-and-a-half week residential program allows students to learn more about various fields, including art. Recent arts-related courses included Photography as Art and Engineering and Design. Although high school credit is not universally granted for participation in the program, some school districts have granted such credit to participating students. The program fee is approximately $2,450 (which includes tuition, room and board, books, and supplies). Some financial aid is available.

Gifted and highly motivated high school students who have completed the grades 10 or 11 can participate in SMU's College Experience Program. The five-week residential program allows students to experience college-level instruction and earn up to six college credits. Students take courses (art, history, psychology, and other areas) from SMU's regular class schedule and also participate in an intensive interdisciplinary study. Applicants must submit an academic transcript, recommendations, an essay, and PSAT, SAT, or ACT scores. Tuition for the program is approximately $1,900; an additional $1,300 for room and board is required.

Southern Methodist University

Summer Programs
PO Box 750383
Dallas, TX 75275-0383
214-768-0123
http://www.smu.edu/continuing_
education/youth

Volunteer Opportunities at the Denver Art Museum

Employment and Internship Opportunities/Field Experience

The Denver Art Museum offers a variety of volunteer opportunities to people of all ages. Volunteers may take on short-term projects as community volunteers, work as staff aides, or join one of the following volunteer councils: conservation, education, flower, information and membership, and museum shop. Visit the museum's Web site to download an application and get further information on possible duties.

Denver Art Museum
Manager of Volunteer Office
100 West 14th Avenue Parkway
Denver, CO 80204-2788
720-865-5045
http://www.denverartmuseum.org

Volunteer Opportunities at the Phoenix Art Museum

Field Experience

Answer questions from museum members, help with tours, and sign up new members. These are just a few of the important duties you might have as a museum volunteer at the Phoenix Art Museum. Visit the museum's Web site to download an application and to get further information on possible duties.

Phoenix Art Museum
Volunteer Office
1625 North Central Avenue
Phoenix, AZ 85004
602-307-2009
volunteer@phxart.org
http://www.phxart.org/getinvolved/volunteer.asp

Volunteer Programs at the Art Institute of Chicago

Field Experience

The Art Institute of Chicago, one of the preeminent art museums in the United States, offers a variety of volunteer opportunities to people of all ages (who must also be members of the Institute). Public-contact volunteers greet visitors, describe daily programs and lectures, give directions, escort VIP groups, sell and renew memberships, and work at special events. Behind-the-scenes volunteers assist in curatorial and administrative offices by answering phones, photocopying, filing, entering data, performing research, and translating materials. Visit the Institute's Web site to download an application.

The Art Institute of Chicago
Manager of Volunteer Programs
111 South Michigan Avenue
Chicago, IL 60603-6110
312-443-3504
mmitchell4@artic.edu
http://www.artic.edu/aic/aboutus/volunteer.html

Read a Book

When it comes to finding out about art, don't overlook a book. (You're reading one now, after all.) What follows is a short, annotated list of books and periodicals related to art. The books range from biographies of well-known artists, to books about what it's like to be an artist, to professional volumes on specific topics. Don't be afraid to check out the professional journals, either. The technical stuff may be way above your head right now, but if you take the time to become familiar with one or two, you're bound to pick up some of what is important to artists, not to mention begin to feel like a part of their world.

This section includes listings for recent materials as well as old favorites. Always check for the latest editions, and, if you find an author you like, ask your librarian to help you find more.

❏ BOOKS

All about Techniques in Illustration. Hauppauge, N.Y.: Barron's Educational Series, 2001. Using black and white and color media, this book shows students how to professionally complete illustrations for advertising, books, and more.

Barrie, Bruner F. *A Sculptor's Guide to Tools and Materials.* Boca Raton, Fla.: A.B.F.S. Publishing, 1998. Detailed overview of everything you will encounter when sculpting—including a helpful Frequently Asked Questions section at the end of each chapter. A useful resource for the beginning sculptor.

Batchelor, David. *Minimalism.* Movements in Modern Art. New York: Cambridge University Press, 1997. An introduction to the style in general, including a discussion about differences among some of its more well-known practitioners, common criticism, and how it has affected subsequent art.

Bates, Jane K. *Becoming an Art Teacher.* Belmont, Calif.: Wadsworth, 2000. A helpful introduction to the field of art education. Shows the reader what it takes to go from student to art teacher.

Beckett, Wendy. *Sister Wendy's 1000 Masterpieces.* London, U.K.: Dorling Kindersley Publishing, 1999. Alphabetical list (by artist) of masterpieces handpicked and narrated by the author. Sister Wendy touches on each artist's technique, symbolism, and inspiration.

Behr, Shulamith. *Expressionism.* Movements in Modern Art. New York: Cambridge University Press, 2000. An overview of the movement that includes historical influences and the works of both well-known and lesser-known artists.

Bomford, David. *Conservation of Paintings.* New Haven, Conn.: National Gallery Publications Ltd., 1998. Informative guide on the main types of conservation treatments of panel and canvas paintings, as well as the different approaches to art restoration through the years.

Bradley, Fiona. *Surrealism.* Movements in Modern Art. New York: Cambridge University Press, 1997. A survey of surrealism, including the prominent artists of the movement, their relationships with one another, and influences on their work.

Camenson, Blythe. *Great Jobs for Art Majors.* 2nd ed. New York: McGraw-Hill, 2003. Gives helpful tips and insight on career opportunities for art majors. Also includes salary statistics, career outlooks, and networking resources.

Causey, Andrew. *Sculpture Since 1945.* Oxford History of Art. New York: Oxford University Press, 1998. Numerous illustrations complement this overview of the evolution of sculpture since the end of World War II.

Cottington, David. *Cubism and Its Histories.* Critical Perspectives in Art History. Manchester, U.K.: Manchester University Press, 2005. Narratives and illustrations that help explain how Cubism fits into modern art and its wide-reaching impact.

Cox, Mary, ed. *2006 Artist's & Graphic Designer's Market.* Cincinnati, Ohio: Writer's Digest Books, 2004. Important resource published annually for artists and designers, with more than 2,300 industry contacts. Contact information includes submission requirements, payment policies, Web sites, and other guidelines. Also includes valuable articles and tips from industry pros. Updated annually.

Cumming, Robert. *Great Artists: The Lives of 50 Painters Explored through Their Work.* London, U.K.: Dorling Kindersley Publishing, 1998. Artists and their most famous work are presented chronologically, detailing their techniques and symbolism, as well as their impact on the art world. A helpful index lists artists, styles, time periods, and major works.

Davies, Penelope J. E., Walter B. Denny, Frima Fox Hofrichter, Joseph F. Jacobs, Ann M. Roberts, and David L. Simon, eds. *Janson's History of Art: Western Tradition.* 7th ed. Upper Saddle River, N.J.: Prentice Hall, 2006. One of the classics of art history, the newly revised edition of this book introduces readers to art styles from Ancient Egypt to the rich history of Western styles in painting, drawing, architecture, and photography.

De Coppet, Laura, and Alan Jones. *The Art Dealers: The Powers Behind the Scene Tell How the Art World Really Works.* Rev. ed. Lanham, Md.: Cooper Square Press, 2002. Fifty-five interviews with New York art dealers, from the 1940s to present, reveal how the art world really operates and the interaction between galleries and artists.

Edwards, Betty. *New Drawing on the Right Side of the Brain Workbook: Guided Practice in the Five Basic Skills of Drawing.* New York: Jeremy P. Tarcher, 2002.

Forty exercises are presented that cover the five basic skills of drawing. This book focuses largely on portraits done in pencil, but also touches on other subject matter and mediums.

Fleishman, Michael. *Starting Your Career as a Freelance Illustrator or Graphic Designer.* New York: Watson-Guptill Publications, 2001. Shows readers how to analyze what markets are right for their work, how to land those jobs, and how to prepare a winning portfolio, make contacts, price one's work, order supplies and equipment, and more. Also covers important Internet tools for illustrators and graphic designers.

Foster, Hal, Rosalind Krauss, Yve-Alain Bois, and Benjamin Buchloh. *Art Since 1900: Modernism, Antimodernism, Postmodernism.* New York: Thames & Hudson, 2005. This collection of short essays provides an engaging and comprehensive study of art in the 20th century.

Frost, Lee. *The A-Z of Creative Photography: Over 70 Techniques Explained in Full.* New York: Watson-Guptill Publications, 1998. Provides techniques and tips to better photography, with color and black and white photos to illustrate each suggestion.

Gair, Angela. *Artist's Manual: A Complete Guide to Painting and Drawing Materials and Techniques.* San Francisco: Chronicle Books, 1996. Informative reference guide on how to work with different mediums—from watercolor to acrylic to charcoal. Also gives tips on composition, color theory, and supplies.

Ganz, Nicholas. *Graffiti World: Street Art from Five Continents.* New York: Harry N. Abrams, 2004. Written by a graffiti artist and illustrated with thousands of photos, this book provides a history of graffiti, interviews with graffiti artists, and a survey of different graffiti styles.

Gombrich, E. H. *The Story of Art.* 16th ed. Boston: Phaidon, 1995. Richly illustrated and written in an easy-to-read and engaging style, this book presents an overview and introduction to Western art from ancient to modern times. Since its publication in 1950, this book has remained one of the best-selling art books of all time.

Grimm, Tom, and Michele Grimm. *Basic Book of Photography.* 5th ed. New York: Plume Books, 2003. Respected handbook for both beginning and experienced photographers. Includes close to 400 instructive illustrations and a glossary, as well as a new chapter on digital cameras and imaging.

Gulrich, Kathy. *187 Tips for Artists: How to Create a Successful Art Career—and Have Fun in the Process!* New York: Center City Publishing, 2003. Award-winning artist and art coach Kathy Gulrich dispenses advice on how to become a more successful artist.

Harrison, Charles. *Modernism.* Movements in Modern Art. New York: Cambridge University Press, 1997. This overview of modernism presents the key characteristics of the movement, and how they are manifested in individual works.

Hodges, Elaine R. S. *The Guild Handbook of Scientific Illustration.* 2nd ed. Hoboken, N.J.: John Wiley & Sons, 2003. Long considered "the bible" of scientific illustration by industry professionals, this book covers all aspects of this specialized field, from 3-D modeling to copyright advice.

Hoving, Thomas. *Art For Dummies.* New York: IDG Books Worldwide, 1999. A no-nonsense tour of the world's best works of art by Thomas Hoving, former director of the Metropolitan Museum of Art.

Humphreys, Richard. *Futurism.* Movements in Modern Art. New York: Cambridge University Press, 1999. Explores the influence of this avant-garde movement, primarily in Europe and Russia, during the 20th century.

Hunter, Sam, Daniel Wheeler, and John M. Jacobus. *Modern Art: Painting, Sculpture, Architecture.* 3rd ed. New York: Prentice Hall, 2000. An intelligently written overview of modern art in Europe and the United States during the 20th century.

Illian, Clary. *A Potter's Workbook.* Iowa City: University of Iowa Press, 1999. Explores the principle of good form and good forming techniques needed to create utilitarian pottery. Also includes useful exercises and illustrations.

Jones, Sue Jenkyn. *Fashion Design.* New York: Watson-Guptill Publications, 2002. Gives the who, what, where, why, and when to all aspects of this competitive industry. A definitive resource guide to anyone interested in a career in fashion.

Joselit, David. *American Art Since 1945.* World of Art. New York: Thames & Hudson, 2003. This survey follows the evolution of American art from mid-20th century on, and the influence of society and culture on it.

Leal, Brigitte, Christine Piot, Marie-Laure Bernadac, and Jean Leymarie. *The Ultimate Picasso.* New York: Harry N. Abrams, 2000. This comprehensive study of Picasso's work is filled with more than 1,000 reproductions.

Leland, Nita. *Exploring Color.* Cincinnati, Ohio: North Light Books, 1998. Beginner-friendly book that details the study of color. Explores the history, theory, and artistic uses of color, and suggests exercises and projects to illustrate them.

Lerner, Ralph E., and Judith Bresler. *Art Law: The Guide for Collectors, Investors, Dealers, and Artists.* 2nd ed. New York: Practising Law Institute, 1998. A large, comprehensive guide to everything you need to know when buying or selling artwork.

London, Barbara, John Upton, Kenneth Kobre, and Betsy Brill. *Photography.* 8th ed. Upper Saddle River, N.J.: Prentice Hall, 2001. Teaches beginners how to use techniques and visual awareness to hone their craft. Also includes detailed instruction on digital imaging and other technological advances.

Malchiodi, Cathy A. *Handbook of Art Therapy.* New York: The Guilford Press, 2002. Thirty case-based chapters show the wide range of settings in which art therapy is applied, from treatment for alcohol abuse to depression. Includes more than 100 examples of client drawings and artwork.

Michels, Caroll. *How to Survive and Prosper as an Artist: Selling Yourself Without Selling Your Soul.* 5th ed. New York: Owl Books, 2001. Handbook filled with information and advice for artists trying to market their work without losing their artistic principles.

Moore, Sean. *How to Make Money as an Artist.* Chicago: Chicago Review Press, 2000. Straightforward guide on how to sell yourself—and your art. Includes a detailed listing of industry resources and contact information for art representation and the media.

National Association of Schools of Art and Design Directory 2004. Reston, Va.: National Association of Schools of Art and Design. Annual publication that lists accredited art institutions and degree programs.

Nauman, Bruce. *Please Pay Attention Please: Bruce Nauman's Words: Writings and Interviews.* Writing Art. Cambridge, Mass.: MIT Press, 2003. A compilation of the installation artist's interviews over a 40-year span, his writings, and illustrations provide an overview of Nauman's style of merging language and art.

Nicholl, Charles. *Leonardo da Vinci: Flights of the Mind: A Biography.* New York: Viking Adult, 2004. An illustrated biography of one of history's most fascinating men.

Olver, Elizabeth. *The Art of Jewelry Design: From Idea to Reality.* Cincinnati, Ohio: North Light Books, 2002. Gives readers techniques and advice on how to transform jewelry designs to reality. Details materials, tools, designs, and functions.

Pope, Alice, and Rebecca Chrysler, eds. *2005 Children's Writer's & Illustrator's Market.* Cincinnati, Ohio: Writer's Digest Books, 2003. Annual publication that includes hundreds of contacts and guideline information for children's magazines and book publishers. Also features interviews with industry veterans.

Preble, Duane, Sarah Preble, and Patrick L. Frank. *Artforms: An Introduction to the Visual Arts.* 7th ed. Upper Saddle River, N.J.: Prentice Hall, 2001. Readers are given new insight to the visual arts by introducing or expanding upon their knowledge of art history, theory, and practice. This latest edition also offers a companion Web site that integrates online learning along with the written text.

Reed, Walt. *The Illustrator in America, 1860-2000.* 3rd ed. New York: Harper Design, 2003. Covers 650 artists from the Civil War to the 20th century, each with a detailed biographical sketch and timeline of influential schools and styles. Includes beautiful color reproductions of each artist's work.

Robinson, Roxana. *Georgia O'Keeffe: A Life.* Lebanon, N.H.: University Press of New England, 1998. The compelling biography of one the most prominent female artists of the 20th century.

Sammon, Rick. *Rick Sammon's Complete Guide to Digital Photography: 107 Lessons on Taking, Making, Editing, Storing, Printing, and Sharing Better Digital Images.* New York: W. W. Norton & Company, 2003. Digital photography advice from one of North America's most widely read photo columnists. More than 1,000 images that detail shooting and Photoshop techniques.

Schaub, George. *Using Your Camera: A Basic Guide to 35mm Photography.* Rev. ed. New York: Amphoto Books, 2002. Excellent beginner's guide, covering topics such as camera functions, composition, and different light exposures.

Scotchie, Virginia. *Setting Up Your Ceramic Studio: Ideas & Plans from Working Artists.* Asheville, N.C.: Lark Books, 2003. Ten actual ceramic studios are described as examples of how each workspace meets a particular artist's needs. Lighting, storage, ventilation, and flooring are some requirements discussed.

Slade, Catharine. *The Encyclopedia of Illustration Techniques.* Philadelphia: Running Press, 1997. Step-by-step directory of illustration techniques. Covers a vast range of mediums, from line drawing to computer illustration.

Smith, Constance. *Art Marketing 101: A Handbook for the Fine Artist.* 2d ed. Cincinnati, Ohio: North Light Books, 2000. Readers are privy to the business and marketing secrets of successful artists. A must-have, user-friendly guide to making it in the art world.

Staff of Andy Warhol Museum. *Andy Warhol 365 Takes: The Andy Warhol Museum Collection.* New York: Harry N. Abrams, 2004. Illustrations, commentaries, and some of Warhol's own writings present a fascinating overview of this contemporary art icon's life and work.

Stevens, Mar, and Annalyn Swan. *De Kooning: An American Master.* New York: Knopf, 2004. A beautifully illustrated biography of this abstract expressionist that provides detail of his personal life and how it affected his art.

Stokstad, Marilyn. *Art History.* 2d ed. Upper Saddle River, N.J.: Prentice Hall, 2004. Beautiful two-volume set details the history of art from prehistoric to modern times. Timelines and more than 1,600 illustrations complement the author's engaging narrative.

Thomson, Belinda. *Impressionism: Origins, Practice, Reception.* World of Art. New York: Thames & Hudson, 2000. An illustrated historical overview of the impressionist movement that looks at the artists, their lives, and the development of the movement, as well as how impressionist works fare in the art world today.

_____. *Post-Impressionism.* Movements in Modern Art. New York: Cambridge University Press, 1998. A survey of the postimpressionist artists, their work, and the stylistic differences that evolved from impressionism.

❏ PERIODICALS

AIC News. Published bimonthly by the American Institute for Conservation of Historic and Artistic Works, 1717 K Street, NW, Suite 200, Washington, DC 20006, http://aic.stanford.edu/library/print/news. Offers news on national and international conservation issues, job listings, tips on new techniques, and information on continuing education opportunities. Available to Institute members only.

American Artist. Published monthly by *American Artist,* 770 Broadway, New York, NY 10003, 866-851-6574, Info@MyAmericanArtist.com, http://www.myamericanartist.com/americanartist/index.jsp. Offers tips, advice, and resources for representational and figurative artists.

American Artist Drawing. Published quarterly by *American Artist,* 770 Broadway, New York, NY 10003, 866-851-6574, Info@MyAmericanArtist.com, http://www.myamericanartist.com/americanartist/index.jsp. Offers ideas and techniques for people who are interested in drawing.

American Craft. Published bimonthly by the American Craft Council (ACC), 72 Spring Street, 6th Floor, New York, NY 10012-4019, 212-274-0630, council@craftcouncil.org, http://www.craftcouncil.org/html/magazine/main.shtml. Features profiles of craft artists (who work with clay, fiber, metal, glass, wood, and other materials) and stories on exhibitions and developments in the field. Available to members of the ACC.

American Educator. Quarterly professional journal of the American Federation of Teachers, AFT Order Department, 555 New Jersey Avenue, NW, Washington, DC 20001, http://www.aft.org/pubs-reports/american_educator. Covers a wide variety of professional issues for K-12 educators (including art teachers).

American Teacher. Published monthly by the American Federation of Teachers, AFT Order Department, 555 New Jersey Avenue, NW, Washington, DC 20001, http://www.aft.org/pubs-reports/american_teacher/index.htm. Covers a wide variety of issues of interest to K-12 educators (including art teachers).

ART + Auction. Published monthly by LTB Holding, 11 East 36th Street, 9th Floor, New York, NY 10016, 800-777-8718, http://www.artandauction.com. Features articles about the art market, including profiles of art collectors, auction news, art transaction prices, and market trends.

The Art Bulletin. Published quarterly by the College Art Association (CAA), CAA Publications, 275 Seventh Avenue, New York, NY 10001, 212-691-1051, ext. 12, memsvcs@collegeart.org, http://www.collegeart.org/artbulletin. Scholarly journal for art historians that covers all areas and periods of art history. Available to CAA members only.

ARTFORUM. Published 10 times annually by *Artforum International Magazine,* Artforum Subscriptions, Box 3000, Denville, NJ 07834, 212-475-4000, http://www.artforum.com.

Provides news about the art world, reviews, interviews with artists, and a calendar of art exhibits and events.

Art in America. Monthly publication that provides in-depth coverage of a wide variety of artistic disciplines (such as painting, sculpture, and photography). Considered one of the most definitive publications available about art today. Subscriptions include a copy of the *Annual Guide to Galleries, Museums, and Artists.* For more information, call 212-941-2806 or visit http://www.artinamericamagazine.com.

Art Journal. Published quarterly by the College Art Association (CAA), CAA Publications, 275 Seventh Avenue, New York, NY 10001, 212-691-1051, ext. 12, memsvcs@collegeart.org, http://www.collegeart.org/artjournal. Offers scholarly articles, interviews, portfolios, and other features about 20th- and 21st-century art.

ARTnews. Published 11 times a year, *ARTnews* offers profiles of artists, collectors, and dealers; previews and reviews of art gallery and museum exhibits; and information on trends, issues, and happenings in the art world. For more information, contact: *ARTnews,* 48 West 38th Street, New York, NY 10018, Tel: 212-398-1690, info@artnewsonline.com, http://www.artnewsonline.com.

Art Therapy: Journal of the American Art Therapy Association. Quarterly publication of the American Art Therapy Association, Inc., 1202 Allanson Road, Mundelein, IL 60060-3808, 888-290-0878, info@arttherapy.org, http://www.arttherapy.org/aaatj.html. Scholarly journal that examines how visual art is used to treat the physically or mentally ill.

CAA News. Bimonthly newsletter of the College Art Association (CAA), CAA Publications, 275 Seventh Avenue, New York, NY 10001. Offers information on trends in art and art history, funding opportunities, member achievements and activities, and other issues in the arts. Visit http://www.collegeart.org/news to read sample articles.

caa.reviews. Online publication of the College Art Association (CAA). Offers reviews of books, exhibitions, digital productions, films, videos, studies, and projects in art, art history, and architecture. Available to CAA members only. To read review excerpts, visit http://www.caareviews.org.

Gain. Online journal of the American Institute of Graphic Arts that provides information on the connections between design and business. Features interviews with business leaders, a column on intellectual property law, and stories about and interviews with well-known designers. Read an issue online at http://gain.aiga.org.

GNSI Journal of Scientific Illustration. Published quarterly by the Guild of Natural Science Illustrators (GNSI), PO Box 652, Ben Franklin Station, Washington, DC 20044-0652, gnsi-home@his.com, http://www.gnsi.org/join/publicat.html#journal. Covers a wide variety of topics that are of interest to scientific illustrators.

GNSI Newsletter. Published 10 times annually by the Guild of Natural Science Illustrators (GNSI), PO Box 652, Ben Franklin Station, Washington, DC 20044-0652, gnsihome@his.com, http://www.gnsi.org/join/publicat. html#newsletter. Features articles on illustration techniques, legal/business issues, exhibits, workshops, and publication reviews. Also features the artwork of Guild members.

Journal of Art Education. Published bimonthly by the National Art Education Association, 1916 Association Drive, Reston, VA 20191-1590, http://www.naea-reston.org. Offers information on trends in art education and job listings for art educators and administrators at the elementary, secondary, and university levels, as well as those employed by libraries and museums.

Journal of the American Institute for Conservation. Published three times annually by the American Institute for Conservation of Historic and Artistic Works, 1717 K Street, NW, Suite 200, Washington, DC 20006, http://aic. stanford.edu/library/print/jaic/jsubsc. html. Offers scholarly articles that cover current issues and trends, scientific research, and technical procedures in the field of conservation. Materials discussed include archeological objects, ethnographic materials, architectural objects, books, paper, paintings, sculpture, photographs, and wooden artifacts.

NCECA News. Published quarterly by the National Council on Education for the Ceramic Arts, 77 Erie Village Square, Suite 280, Erie, CO 80516-6996, 866-266-2322, http://www. nceca.net/publications/newsletter. html. Member publication that offers updates on council events and serves as a forum for member ideas and thoughts on the ceramic arts.

NEA ARTS. Bimonthly newsletter published by the National Endowment for the Arts (NEA). Covers the NEA's national initiatives and programs, awards, and grants. Also includes a calendar of NEA events. Available online (http://www.arts.gov/about/ NEARTS/index.html) only in PDF format.

News Photographer Magazine. Published monthly by the National Press Photographers Association, 6677 Whitemarsh Valley Walk, Austin, TX 78746-6367, magazine@nppa.org. Offers articles about current trends in the industry, profiles of well-known photojournalists, and tips on equipment and gear. Selected articles are available at http://www.nppa.org/ news_and_events/magazine.

Professional Photographer. Published monthly by the Professional Photographers of America, 229 Peachtree Street, NE, Suite 2200, International Tower, Atlanta, GA 30303, 800-742-7468, ppa@bframe.com. Offers useful information for aspiring and practicing photographers. Includes business and artistic tips, equipment and technology profiles, interviews with well-known photographers, and industry information.

Sculpture. Published monthly by the International Sculpture Center, 1529 18th Street, NW, Washington, DC 20036, 202-234-0555, isc@sculpture.org. Covers issues and trends in contemporary sculpture. Also includes profiles of artists, exhibit reviews, and job listings. Visit http://www.sculpture.org/redesign/mag.shtml to read selected articles.

Sculpture Review. Published quarterly by the National Sculpture Society, 56 Ludlow Street, 5th Floor, New York, NY 10002, 212-529-1763, GP@SculptureReview.com, http://www.sculpturereview.com. Features interviews with well-known sculptors, news about trends, book reviews, and profiles of rising artists in the field.

Voice: AIGA Journal of Design. American Institute of Graphic Arts. Online journal of the American Institute of Graphic Arts. Offers useful articles about trends and issues in graphic design. Also offers an online forum that readers can use to share their ideas or feedback regarding articles. You can read the publication by visiting http://journal.aiga.org/.

Watercolor. Published quarterly by *American Artist,* 770 Broadway, New York, NY 10003, 866-851-6574, Info@MyAmericanArtist.com, http://www.myamericanartist.com/americanartist/index.jsp. Offers ideas and techniques for watercolor enthusiasts.

Surf the Web

The World Wide Web offers a wealth of information on art and often does it in a way where you can actually have fun while learning. This gets you started with an annotated list of Web sites related to art and art careers. The more you read about and interact with artists, the better prepared you'll be when you're old enough to participate as a professional.

One caveat: you probably already know that URLs change all the time. If a Web address listed below is out of date, try searching on the site's name or other key words. Chances are, if it's still out there, you'll find it. If it's not, maybe you'll find something better.

❏ THE LIST

About: Art History
http://arthistory.about.com

The popular Internet search engine About.com offers useful resources for students, art teachers, and art history buffs. Skip the main page and look instead to the menu on the left side of the screen. For information on the fly, check out 60-Second Artist Profiles or Famous Names in Art. Both sections allow you to browse artists by last name and offer short profiles about the person and their work. The Timelines of Art History section is also useful to get a sense of the time periods in which artists worked.

About: Drawing/Sketching
http://drawsketch.about.com

In addition to its art history section, About.com also offers this site for those interested in illustration. The Essentials area hosts articles and lessons on drawing, including recommended supplies, how to get started, and drawing hints and tips. Beginner courses cover all the basics from how to sketch a still-life to drawing live models. The best part? The site and its services are free. You can explore at your own pace and backtrack or skip ahead at any time.

Admiral Cowdisley Education Group
http://www.cowdisley.com

This site was created by a group of senior professional artists who want to pass on their appreciation of art to others. The best parts of this site are the illustrated, online art lessons for beginning and advanced fine art students. The site includes lessons in theory, practice, and art appreciation. This is a useful site for the aspiring artist who might not have the means or time to take conventional lessons.

Albright-Knox ArtGames

http://www.albrightknox.org/artgames

Created by an art gallery in Buffalo, New York, this interactive site tests your knowledge of famous works of art and painting styles through games. Follow "Artie" through the series of lessons and see how much you learned by taking the quiz. From Seurat's pointillism to Gris' abstract art, this site is fun to browse and educational at the same time.

Antiques Roadshow

http://www.pbs.org/wgbh/pages/roadshow

By now, you're probably familiar with the popular PBS show *Antiques Roadshow,* where art experts examine family treasures or rummage sale bargains for hidden gems. This Web site offers information about the television show, tips for appraising art and antiques, and a list of useful books about various types of art. The Follow the Stories section offers articles about antiques and the pieces covered on the show. It includes a discussion of the detective work that is often necessary to discover fakes and forgeries as well as hidden masterpieces.

Art History Resources on the Web

http://witcombe.sbc.edu/ARTHLinks.html

Created by a professor of art history at Sweet Briar College in Virginia, this site offers links to information on various eras and movements. From early prehistoric times to the 21st century, each sec-tion offers Web links to sites on the time period plus lists of artists popular during that period.

The Art Institute of Chicago: Art Access

http://www.artic.edu/artaccess

This site studies objects from the Art Institute of Chicago's permanent collection to "enrich visitors' understanding of their content, style, and historical context." Major areas covered include: African American Art; American Art to 1900; Ancient Indian Art of the Americas; Impressionism and Post-Impressionism; India, Himalayas, and Southeast Asia; Modern and Contemporary Art; and Renaissance and Baroque Art. The Web site also offers lesson plans for teachers, art projects that you can work on at home, glossaries, and suggested books and media.

The Art Institute of Chicago: Science, Art &Technology

http://www.artic.edu/aic/students/onlinelearning.html

This Web site offers a fascinating look at the relationship between science and art in a museum setting. Art historians, museum educators, conservators, artists, scientists, and other museum professionals talk about the intersection of science and art via videos, articles, and lesson plans for teachers. For example, a conservation microscopist discusses how microscopy is used to authenticate and evaluate the condition of art, a professor discusses the mathematical system of linear perspective, and an art conservator discusses the scientific methods used to attribute a previously unknown painting in the institute's collection to a well-known artist of the 18th century.

The Art Room
http://www.arts.ufl.edu/art/rt_room

Though no longer updated, this site from the Department of Art Education at the University of Florida still contains fun and informational content. Browse through the Gallery, which features artwork from young art students from the United States and around the world. Click on "@rtifacts" to learn interesting facts about famous works, such as how the "Mona Lisa" was stolen and recovered, and how the famous "American Gothic" painting went from public disdain to the prestigious work it is today. Finally, the "@rtrageous Thinking" section encourages you to think like an artist and try art projects of your own.

ArtCyclopedia
http://artcyclopedia.com

Visitors to this site can browse 150,000 works of art from more than 8,000 painters, sculptors, and photographers via links to art museums and image archives throughout the world. You can search by artist's name, title of a work, or art museum. The site also offers brief overviews of major art movements (such as Abstract Expressionism, Minimalism, and Pop Art) and a timeline of key artists working in these disciplines.

Artist Resource: Job Hunting Advice for Designers, Artists, and Illustrators
http://www.artistresource.org/jobhunt.htm

This page is part of a larger site offering everything from job leads to studios for rent. Skip the main part of the site and go directly to this page, which includes some information on select art careers and job tips (which you will need to scroll down to find). Located towards the bottom of this page is some priceless information on preparing for situational interviews and traditional interviews and refining your resume and portfolio to reflect your chosen art specialty.

Artists Foundation: Resources for Artists
http://www.artistsfoundation.org/art_pages/resources/resources.htm

Visit this page from the Artists Foundation, an organization dedicated to promoting artists and strengthening communication between the artist community and the general public. This resource page includes tips on job hunting, how to become an artist, and how to sustain a career.

Under "Being in the Arts," browse topics such as finding an appropriate workspace, protecting your First Amendment rights, and tips on selling your work.

The-Artists.org
http://www.the-artists.org

This site features profiles of modern and contemporary visual artists. Each artist profile offers a brief biography, photographs of their art, and links to articles, essays, and interviews relating to their work. The site also features definitions of various art movements and suggested reading.

ArtResource: Artists' Stories

http://www.artistresource.org/stories. htm

This page of the main ArtResource site is worth exploring like a good book. Included are personal essays, notes from art seminars, and poems written by working artists in the field. At the end of every story is the artist's own portfolio. Perhaps after reading enough of them, you will want to submit one of your own! (Be sure to read the submission guidelines first.)

ArtSchools.com

http://www.artschools.com

This online art school directory, which claims to be the "largest and most popular" search engine of its kind, enables you to search and compare art schools, colleges, workshops, and programs by name or by location. School listings provide contact information, Web and e-mail links, class or program examples, and a short description of what each institution has to offer.

Baltimore Museum of Art: Matisse for Kids

http://www.artbma.org/education/ matisse_kids_frame.html

At first sight, this link may seem aimed solely for young audiences, but the art-curious of all ages will enjoy following Raoudi, the artist Henri Matisse's schnau-

zer, through the site. Learn about the artist's use of props, colors, and patterns through informative lessons, and then collect images from his famous works and put them in your portfolio.

GradSchools.com: Arts and Fine Arts

http://www.gradschools.com/art_ fine.html

This site offers listings of art schools searchable by state. From the home page, use the drop-down menu to choose the concentration of your interest, such as Art/Fine Art, Art History, Art Administration, Art Therapy, or Ceramics. From there use the map to narrow your school search. Listings include program info, degrees offered, school Web site, and e-mail contact.

Imagine

http://www.jhu.edu/~gifted/imagine

Imagine is a bimonthly journal for the go-getter high school student with his or her eye on the future. Its tag line, "Opportunities and resources for academically talented youth," says it all.

If you're always searching for good academic programs, competitions, and internships, this publication can keep you well informed on what's available and when you need to apply. There's an entertaining College Review series in which student contributors evaluate individual colleges and universities and also a Career Options series featuring interviews with professionals.

Along with the current issue, selected portions of back issues can be read online.

Previous issues have included articles about the visual arts, as well as general tips on entering art competitions and choosing summer programs. For $25 a year, you can subscribe and get the printed journal delivered to your home—or for free, you can just read back issues online.

National Museum of Women in the Arts

http://www.nmwa.org

This is the only art museum in the world that focuses solely on the work of female artists. Visit its Web site to view selections from its collection and to learn more about visiting the museum, which is located in Washington, D.C.

New York Foundation for the Arts: Business of Art Articles

http://www.nyfa.org/level2.asp?id=51&fid=1&sid=197

While this site offers much more than these articles, check out this link first for a good one-stop informational clearinghouse on anything from careers, to education, to owning your own business. The Careers link includes interesting reads such as "The Ten Habits of Successful Artists" or "Dr. Art on Dealing with Rejection." Check out the Interviews with Art Professionals link to read Q&A sessions with artists from various disciplines and backgrounds.

Peterson's Education Portal

http://www.petersons.com

This site offers anything you want to know about surviving high school, get-

ting into college, and choosing a graduate degree. Specific to art, check out the College and Grad School sections, which offer school directories searchable by keyword, degree, location, tuition, size, GPA, and even sports. While this site is not devoted to art schools, it is useful for its comprehensiveness. School listings here offer the usual basics plus details on financial aid, school facilities, student government, faculty, and admissions requirements.

Peterson's Guide to Summer Programs for Teenagers

http://www.petersons.com/summerop

Your commitment to a brilliant academic future might waver when you visit this site. Along with some great information about art-focused summer programs, you'll be tantalized by summer camps that revolve around activities that are less mentally rigorous—like white water rafting or touring Switzerland on a bicycle. Shake it off. You're here to further your education, and this site offers good tips on assessing any summer program or camp you're considering.

Finding a camp that suits your interests is easy enough at this site; just search Peterson's database of art programs. Under the Arts heading, you'll find a list of links to dozens of topics, from drawing to glass blowing to painting to printmaking—to name a few. Click on a topic and then a specific program or camp for a quick overview description. In some instances you'll get a more in-depth description, along with photographs, applications, and online brochures. If you need to limit your search to your home state, that's easy enough, too. You can sift through Peterson's database by geographic region or alphabetically.

Princeton Review
http://www.princetonreview.com

Similar to the Peterson's Web site, Princeton Review is a great site to find comprehensive college reviews and information. Unique to this site are actual student comments about the school, which offer refreshingly honest opinions about the institution and its student body. Check out the site's school rankings to read how schools stack up in academics, social scene, diversity, and other areas. Under the Students Tell All section, read about what students have to say about their college experience.

SmART Kids
http://smartmuseum.uchicago.edu/smartkids

Hosted by the David and Alfred Smart Museum of Art, this interactive site invites you to be an art detective and explore the site with a cartoon partner. Each character leads you through online games and activities answering common questions such as how photographs are developed, what makes ordinary objects art, and how to "speak" art.

Smithsonian American Art Museum
http://nmaa-ryder.si.edu

Aside from being one of the leading art museums of the world, the Smithsonian also hosts a great Web site complete with online galleries and exhibitions. If after surfing the site you still have a burning question left unanswered, be sure to visit Ask Joan of Art, which allows you to e-mail the Smithsonian experts with any question you may have about a specific artist, work of art, or other art-related topic.

Yahoo!: Arts
http://dir.yahoo.com/Arts

It might seem odd to include the popular search engine Yahoo! among a list of art Web sites, but it won't seem so after you've visited it. If you're hungry for more after visiting the sites listed in this appendix, pull up a chair at Yahoo!'s feast.

Yahoo! has done a tremendous amount of legwork for you. For example, if you're interested in art history, then scan through more than 1,700 sites currently included here. Museums, galleries, and centers post an impressive 1,000+ sites. Even art therapy offers approximately 40 sites you probably wouldn't have known to look for otherwise. This is a useful starting point for Web research about the arts.

Ask for Money

By the time most students get around to thinking about applying for scholarships, grants, and other financial aid, they have already extolled their personal, academic, and artistic virtues to such lengths in essays, interviews, and portfolios for college applications that even their own grandmothers wouldn't recognize them. The thought of filling out yet another application form fills students with dread. And why bother? Won't the same five or six kids who have been competing for academic and artistic honors for years walk away with all the really good scholarships?

The truth is, most of the scholarships available to high school and college students are being offered because an organization wants to promote interest in a particular field, encourage more students to become qualified to enter it, and finally, to help those students afford an education. Certainly, having a great portfolio or good grade point average is a valuable asset. More often than not, however, grade point averages aren't even mentioned; the focus is on the area of interest and what a student has done to distinguish himself or herself in that area. In fact, sometimes the only requirement is that the scholarship applicant must be studying in a particular area.

❏ GUIDELINES

When applying for scholarships there are a few simple guidelines that can help ease the process considerably.

Plan Ahead

The absolute worst thing you can do is wait until the last minute. For one thing, obtaining recommendations or other supporting data in time to meet an application deadline is incredibly difficult. For another, no one does their best thinking or writing under the gun. So get off to a good start by reviewing scholarship applications as early as possible—months, even a year, in advance. If the current scholarship information isn't available, ask for a copy of last year's version. Once you have the scholarship information or application in hand, give it a thorough read. Try to determine how your experience or situation best fits into the scholarship, or if it even fits at all. Don't waste your time applying for a scholarship in literature if you couldn't finish *Great Expectations*.

If possible, research the award or scholarship, including past recipients and, where applicable, the person in whose name the scholarship is offered. Often, scholarships are established to memorialize an individual who majored in art or who loved history, for example, but in other cases, the scholarship is to memorialize the *work* of an individual. In those cases, try to get a feel for the spirit of the person's work. If you have any similar interests, experiences, or abilities, don't hesitate to mention these.

Talk to others who received the scholarship, or to students currently studying in the same area or field of interest in which the scholarship is offered, and try to gain insight into possible applications or work related to that field. When you're working on the essay asking why you want this scholarship, you'll have real answers such as, "I would benefit from receiving this scholarship because studying art therapy will help me to improve the lives of the physically or mentally ill."

Take your time writing the essays. Make sure you are answering the question or questions on the application and not merely restating facts about yourself. Don't be afraid to get creative; try to imagine what you would think of if you had to sift through hundreds of applications: What would you want to know about the candidate? What would convince you that someone was deserving of the scholarship? Work through several drafts and have someone whose advice you respect—a parent, teacher, or guidance counselor—review the essay for grammar and content.

Finally, if you know in advance which scholarships you want to apply for, there might still be time to stack the deck in your favor by getting an internship, volunteering, or working part time. Bottom line: the more you know about a scholarship and the sooner you learn it, the better.

Follow Directions

Think of it this way: many of the organizations that offer scholarships devote 99.9 percent of their time to something other than the scholarship for which you are applying. Don't make a nuisance of yourself by pestering them for information. Simply follow the directions as they are presented to you. If the scholarship application specifies that you write for further information, then write for it—don't call.

Pay close attention to whether you're applying for an award, a scholarship, a prize, or financial aid. Often these words are used interchangeably, but just as often they have different meanings. An award is usually given for something you have done (helping to build a park or distribute meals to the elderly) or something you have created (a work of art, a design, an essay, a short film, a screenplay, or an invention). On the other hand, a scholarship is frequently a renewable sum of money that is given to a person to help defray the costs of college. Scholarships are given to candidates who meet the necessary criteria based on artistic ability, essays, eligibility, grades, or sometimes all four.

Supply all the necessary documents, information, and fees, and make the deadlines. You won't win any scholarships by forgetting to include a recommendation from a teacher or failing to postmark the application by the deadline. Bottom line: get it right the first time, on time.

Apply Early

Once you have the application in hand, don't dawdle. If you've requested it far enough in advance, there shouldn't be any reason for you not to turn it well in advance of the deadline. You never know—if it comes down to two candidates, your timeliness just might be the deciding factor. Bottom line: don't wait.

Be Yourself

Don't make promises you can't keep. There are plenty of hefty scholarships available, but if they all require you to study something that you don't enjoy, you'll be miserable in college. And the side effects from switching majors after you've accepted a scholarship could be even worse. Bottom line: be yourself.

Don't Limit Yourself

There are many sources for scholarships, beginning with your guidance counselor and ending with the Internet. All of the search engines have education categories. Start there and search by keywords such as *financial aid, scholarship,* and *award.* But don't be limited to the scholarships listed in these pages.

If you know of an organization related to or involved with the field of your choice, write a letter asking if they offer scholarships. If they don't offer scholarships, don't stop there. Write them another letter, or better yet, schedule a meeting with the president or someone in the public relations office and ask them if they would be willing to sponsor a scholarship for you. Of course, you'll need to prepare yourself well for such a meeting because you're selling a priceless commodity—yourself. Don't be shy—be confident. Tell them all about yourself, what you want to study and why, and let them know what you would

be willing to do in exchange: volunteer at their favorite charity, write up reports on your progress in school, or work part time on school breaks or full time during the summer. Explain why you're a wise investment. Bottom line: the sky's the limit.

❏ THE LIST

American Indian Arts Council
725 Preston Forest Shopping Center, Suite B
Dallas, TX 75230

Native American high school students who are planning to pursue careers in the visual arts may apply for $250 to $1,000 scholarships. Applicants must provide documentation that verifies their Native American heritage. Contact the council by mail for more information.

Appraisers Association of America
386 Park Avenue South, Suite 2000
New York, NY 10016
212-889-5404
appraisers@appraisersassoc.org
http://www.appraisersassoc.org

College students enrolled in an appraisal studies program may apply for the $1,000 Augustus H. Fisher Fellowship. Visit the association's Web site for further information.

Association on American Indian Affairs
Scholarship Coordinator
966 Hungerford Drive, Suite 12-B
Rockville, MD 20850
240-314-7155

general.aaia@verizon.net
http://www.indian-affairs.org

Undergraduate and graduate Native American students who are pursuing a wide variety of college majors (including art) can apply for several different scholarships ranging from $500 to $1,500. All applicants must provide proof of Native American heritage. Visit the association's Web site for more information.

California Alliance for Arts Education

495 East Colorado Boulevard
Pasadena, CA 91101
626-578-9315
eyaa@artsed411.org
http://www.artsed411.org/projects/eya.stm

Young artists pursuing postsecondary training in visual arts are eligible to apply for Emerging Young Artist Awards of up to $5,000 per year for four years. Applicants must be high school seniors, demonstrate financial need, and reside in the state of California. For further details and to download an application, visit the alliance's Web site. Many other states have similar organizations, but they may not offer scholarships or grants to aspiring artists. Visit http://www.kennedy-center.org/education/kcaaen/statealliance/aaemem.html for a list of programs in your state or search the Web using keywords such as *state art councils* or *state art alliances*.

College Art Association

275 Seventh Avenue
New York, NY 10001
212-691-1051

nyoffice@collegeart.org
http://www.collegeart.org/fellowships

Students pursuing graduate study in the arts may apply for $5,000 and $10,000 Professional Development Fellowships. Special consideration will be given to applicants who demonstrate financial need and/or who are "underrepresented in their field due to race, religion, gender, age, national origin, sexual orientation, disability, or financial status." Visit the Association's Web site for eligibility requirements and downloadable applications.

Collegeboard.com

http://apps.collegeboard.com/cbsearch_ss/welcome.jsp

This testing service (PSAT, SAT, and so forth) also offers a scholarship search engine. It features scholarships (not all art-related) worth more than $3 billion. You can search by specific major and a variety of other criteria.

CollegeNET

http://mach25.collegenet.com/cgi-bin/M25/index

CollegeNET features 600,000 scholarships (not all art-related) worth more than $1.6 billion. You can search by keyword or by creating a personality profile of your interests.

FastWeb

http://fastweb.monster.com

FastWeb features 600,000 scholarships (not all art-related) worth over $1 billion. To use this resource, you will need to register (for free).

Florida Alliance for Arts Education/Arts for a Complete Education

The First Lady's Arts Recognition
   Scholarship Program
402 Office Plaza
Tallahassee, FL 32301-2757
http://www.faae.org

High school seniors planning to major in the arts are eligible to apply for Arts Recognition Scholarships. Applicants must be Florida residents. Visit the alliance's Web site for more information. Many other states have similar organizations, but they may not offer scholarships or grants to aspiring artists. Visit http://www.kennedy-center.org/education/kcaaen/statealliance/aaemem.html for a list of programs in your state or search the Web using keywords such as *state art councils* or *state art alliances.*

Foundation for the Carolinas

PO Box 34769
Charlotte, NC 28234
704-973-4500
infor@fftc.org
http://www.fftc.org

The Foundation administers more than 70 scholarship funds that offer awards to undergraduate and graduate students pursuing study in the arts and other disciplines. Visit its Web site for a searchable list of awards.

Golden Key International Honor Society

PO Box 23737
Nashville, TN 37202-3737
800-377-2401
htttp://www.goldenkey.org

Golden Key is an academic honor society that offers its members "opportunities for individual growth through leadership, career development, networking, and service." It awards more than $400,000 in scholarships annually through 17 different award programs. Membership in the Society is selective; only the top 15 percent of college juniors and seniors—who may be pursuing education in any college major—are considered for membership by the organization. There is a one-time membership fee of $60 to $65. Contact the Society for more information.

GuaranteedScholarships.com

http://www.guaranteed-scholarships.com

This Web site offers lists (by college) of scholarships, grants, and financial aid (not all art-related) that "require no interview, essay, portfolio, audition, competition, or other secondary requirement."

Hawaii Community Foundation

1164 Bishop Street, Suite 800
Honolulu, HI 96813
scholarships@hcf-hawaii.org
http://www.hawaiicommunityfoundation.org/scholar/scholar.php

The foundation offers a variety of scholarships for high school seniors and college students planning to or currently studying art and other majors in college. Applicants must be residents of Hawaii, demonstrate financial need, and plan to attend a two- or four-year college. Visit the foundation's Web site for more information and to apply online.

Illinois Career Resource Network
http://www.ilworkinfo.com/icrn.htm

Created by the Illinois Department of Employment Security, this useful site offers a great scholarship search engine, as well as detailed information on careers (including art). You can search for art scholarships based on art majors and keywords. This site is available to everyone, not just Illinois residents; you can get a password by simply visiting the site. The Illinois Career Information System is just one example of sites created by state departments of employment security (or departments of labor) to assist students with financial- and career-related issues. After checking out this site, visit your state's department of labor Web site to see what they offer.

Maryland State Arts Council
175 West Ostend Street, Suite E
Baltimore, MD 21230
410-767-6555
msac@msac.org
http://www.msac.org

Maryland artists who are at least 18 years of age may compete for Maryland State Arts Council Individual Artist Awards of $1,000, $3,000, and $6,000. Applicants must be Maryland residents. Students who are currently enrolled in art degree programs are not eligible. Visit the council's Web site and click on "Grants" for details. Many other states have similar organizations, but they may not offer

scholarships or grants to aspiring artists. Visit http://www.kennedy-center.org/education/kcaaen/statealliance/aaemem.html for a list of programs in your state or search the Web using keywords such as *state art councils* or *state art alliances.*

Minnesota State Arts Board
Park Square Court, Suite 200
400 Sibley Street
Saint Paul, MN 55101-1928
msab@arts.state.mn.us
http://www.arts.state.mn.us

The board offers $2,000 to $6,000 grants to Minnesota artists at various stages in their careers. Visit its Web site for more information. Many other states have similar organizations, but they may not offer scholarships or grants to aspiring artists. Visit http://www.kennedy-center.org/education/kcaaen/statealliance/aaemem.html for a list of programs in your state or search the Web using keywords such as *state art councils* or *state art boards.*

National Art Materials Trade Association (NAMTA)
15806 Brookway Drive, Suite 300
Huntersville, NC 28078
704-892-6244
http://www.namta.org

High school seniors and college students planning to or currently majoring in art or art education are eligible to apply for two $2,500 scholarships. The association also offers two $1,500 scholarships to employees or family members of employees of its member-firms. Applicants must be high school seniors or college students. Winners may study art or any other academic major in college. Visit the NAMTA Web site for more information and to download an application.

National Council on Education for the Ceramic Arts
77 Erie Village Square, Suite 280
Erie, CO 80516-6996
866-266-2322
office@nceca.net
http://www.nceca.net/resources/reginab.html

Undergraduate students who have attained at least junior standing are eligible to apply for one of three $1,800 Regina Brown Undergraduate Student Fellowships. Visit the council's Web site for details and an application.

National Endowment for the Arts (NEA)
1100 Pennsylvania Avenue, NW
Washington, DC 20506
202-682-5400
http://arts.endow.gov/grants

The NEA was established by Congress in 1965 to support excellence in the arts. It offers grants to artists and arts organizations working in the following art disciplines: arts education, design, folk and traditional arts, media arts, multidisciplinary, and visual arts. Visit the NEA Web site for a detailed list of available programs.

National Foundation for Advancement in the Arts
Arts Recognition and Talent Search
444 Brickell Avenue, P-14
Miami, FL 33131

800-970-ARTS
http://www.nfaa.org

High school seniors and other 17- and 18-year-old artists are eligible to apply for $3 million in college scholarships via the Arts Recognition and Talent Search. Individual cash awards range from $100 to $10,000. Applicants are not judged against one another, but judged based on standards of excellence established by the foundation. Visit its Web site for more information.

National Sculpture Society (NSS)
237 Park Avenue
New York, NY 10017
212-764-5645
http://www.sculpturereview.com/nss.html

Young sculptors and sculptors in the early stages of their careers can compete in the Society's (co-sponsored by the Lyme Academy of Fine Arts and Pennsylvania Academy of the Fine Arts) National Sculpture Competition. Prizes range from $300 to $1,000 in the two-part competition. Students of figurative or representational sculpture are encouraged to apply for $1,000 scholarships from the Society. Applicants must demonstrate financial need. Contact the NSS for more information.

National Urban League (NUL)
120 Wall Street
New York, NY 10005
info@nul.org
http://www.nul.org
This civil rights organization offers a scholarship in association with the University of Rochester and an extensive list of minor-

ity-focused scholarships from other organizations. Minority high school seniors and undergraduate and graduate students are eligible for these awards. Visit the NUL's Web site for more information.

Nebraska Arts Council
Joslyn Carriage House
3838 Davenport Street
Omaha, NE 68131
800-341-4067
http://www.nebraskaartscouncil.org

The council offers Individual Artist Fellowships of $1,000 to $5,000 to Nebraska visual artists, performing artists, and writers of superior ability. Contact the council for more information. Many other states have similar organizations, but they may not offer scholarships or grants to aspiring artists. Visit http://www.kennedy-center.org/education/kcaaen/statealliance/aaemem.html for a list of programs in your state or search the Web using keywords such as *state art councils* or *state art alliances*.

New York Foundation for the Arts
155 Avenue of the Americas, 14th Floor
New York, NY 10013-1507
212-366-6900, ext. 217
nyfaafp@nyfa.org
http://www.nyfa.org

Artists residing in New York State are eligible for two types of financial aid from the foundation. Artists' Fellowships are $7,000 cash awards that are offered in 16 artistic disciplines (applications are accepted in eight of these categories each year). These include architecture/environmental structures, computer arts, crafts, painting, performance art/multidisciplinary work, photography, printmaking/drawing/artists' books, sculpture, and video. Special Opportunity Stipends are offered to help individual artists from all disciplines "take advantage of unique opportunities that will significantly benefit their work or career development." Awards range from $100 to $600. Visit the NYFA Web site to download an application and for more information.

North Dakota Council on the Arts
1600 East Century Avenue, Suite 6
    Bismarck, ND 58503
701-328-7592
jwebb@state.nd.us
http://www.state.nd.us/arts/grants/grants.htm

The council awards $2,500 Individual Artist Fellowships to practicing artists residing in North Dakota. Visit the council's Web site for more information. Many other states have similar organizations, but they may not offer scholarships or grants to aspiring artists. Visit http://www.kennedy-center.org/education/kcaaen/statealliance/aaemem.html for a list of programs in your state or search the Web using keywords such as *state art councils* or *state art alliances*.

Oklahoma Visual Arts Coalition
PO Box 54416
Oklahoma City, OK 73154
405-232-6991
http://www.ovac-ok.org/artinfogrants.html

The Coalition offers grants and awards to Oklahoma artists who are at least 18 years old and not attending a degree program in visual arts. Awards range from $2,500 to $5,000. Contact the Coalition for more information. Many other states have similar organizations, but they may not offer scholarships or grants to aspiring artists. Visit http://www.kennedy-center.org/education/kcaaen/statealliance/aaemem.html for a list of programs in your state or search the Web using keywords such as *state art councils* or *state art alliances.*

Sallie Mae
http://www.collegeanswer.com

This Web site offers a scholarship database of more than 2.4 million awards (not all art-related) worth more than $14 billion. You must register (free) to use the database.

Scholarship America
One Scholarship Way
St. Peter, MN 56082
800-537-4180
http://www.scholarshipamerica.org

This organization works through its local Dollars for Scholars chapters in 41 states and the District of Columbia. In 2003, it awarded more than $29 million in scholarships to students. Visit Scholarship America's Web site for more information.

Scholarships.com
http://www.scholarships.com

Scholarships.com offers a free college scholarship search engine (registration required) and financial aid information.

Scholastic
c/o Alliance For Young Artists And
    Writers, Inc.
555 Broadway
New York, NY 10012
212-343-6493
a&wgeneralinfo@scholastic.com
http://www.scholastic.com/artandwritingawards

Student-artists and -writers in grades 7 through 12 are eligible to apply for Scholastic Art and Writing Awards of up to $10,000. Art categories for graduating high school seniors include animation, art portfolio, ceramics and glass, computer art, design, digital imagery, drawing, mixed media, painting, photography, photography portfolio, printmaking, sculpture, and video and film. More than $20 million in scholarships have been awarded since the awards were founded in 1923. Visit Scholastic's Web site for a detailed overview of the various awards, competition levels, and application instructions.

UNICO National Inc.
Fairfield Commons
271 US Highway 46 West,
    Suite A-108
Fairfield, NJ 07004
973-808-0035
http://www.unico.org

UNICO touts itself as the largest Italian-American service organization in the United States. High school seniors and college students planning to or currently majoring in fine art are eligible to apply for its $1,500 Theodore Mazza Scholarship. UNICO also offers scholarships that require applicants to be of Italian origin. Visit UNICO's Web site for further details.

United Negro College Fund (UNCF)

http://www.uncf.org/scholarships

Visitors to the UNCF Web site can search for thousands of scholarships and grants, many of which are administered by the UNCF. High school seniors and undergraduate and graduate students are eligible. The search engine allows you to search by art major, state, scholarship title, grade level, and achievement score.

Vermont Alliance for Arts Education

PO Box 327
Fairlee, VT 05045
802-333-4468
vaae@valley.net
http://www.vaae.org

High school seniors planning to major in the arts are eligible to apply for VAAE Student Arts Scholarships. Applicants must be Vermont residents. Visit the Alliance's Web site for more information. Many other states have similar organizations, but they may not offer scholarships or grants to aspiring artists. Visit http://www.kennedy-center.org/education/kcaaen/statealliance/aaemem.html for a list of programs in your state or search the Web using keywords such as *state art councils* or *state art alliances.*

World Studio Foundation

200 Varick Street, Suite 507
New York, NY 10014
scholarshipcoordinator@
    worldstudio.org
http://www.worldstudio.org

High school seniors and college students planning to or currently pursuing undergraduate or graduate degrees in the fine or commercial arts, design, or architecture are eligible to apply for scholarships from the foundation. Scholarships are offered in the following areas: advertising (art direction only), animation, architecture, crafts, environmental graphics, fashion design, film/theater design (costume, set, lighting), film/video (direction or cinematography only), fine arts, furniture design, graphic design, illustration, industrial/product design, interior design, landscape architecture, new media, photography, surface/textile design, and urban planning. Applicants must demonstrate financial need; preference will be given to applicants from underrepresented minority groups. Visit the foundation's Web site for more information on scholarship amounts and to download an application.

Look to the Pros

The following professional organizations offer a variety of materials, from career brochures to lists of accredited schools to salary surveys. Many of them also publish journals and newsletters that you should become familiar with. A number also have annual conferences that you might be able to attend. (While you may not be able to attend a conference as a participant, it may be possible to cover one for your school or even your local paper, especially if your school has a related club.)

When contacting professional organizations, keep in mind that they all exist primarily to serve their members, be it through continuing education, professional licensure, political lobbying, or just "keeping up with the profession." While many are strongly interested in promoting their profession and passing information about it to the general public, these professional organizations are also very busy with other activities. Whether you call or write, be courteous, brief, and to the point. Know what you need and ask for it. If the organization has a Web site, check it out first: what you're looking for may be available there for downloading, or you may find a list of prices or instructions, such as sending a self-addressed, stamped envelope with your request. Finally, be aware that organizations, like people, move. To save time when writing, first confirm the address, preferably with a quick phone call to the organization itself or through a visit to its Web site.

❏ THE SOURCES

American Art Therapy Association (AATA)
1202 Allanson Road
Mundelein, IL 60060-3808
888-290-0878
info@arttherapy.org
http://www.arttherapy.org

This association offers information on art therapy careers, a list of AATA-approved graduate-level programs in art therapy, and links to information on scholarships.

American Association of University Professors
1012 14th Street, NW, Suite 500
Washington, DC 20005
202-737-5900
http://www.aaup.org

Contact the association for information about earnings and union membership for college professors.

American Craft Council
72 Spring Street, 6th Floor
New York, NY 10012-4019

212-274-0630
council@craftcouncil.org
http://www.craftcouncil.org

This national nonprofit educational organization promotes an understanding of American craft. Its Web site offers an overview of craft art, membership opportunities, useful publications, and a list of craft shows and markets. The council also offers a mentor program that prepares artists with no prior wholesale experience to exhibit their work at a wholesale art show.

American Federation
of Teachers (AFT)

555 New Jersey Avenue, NW
Washington, DC 20001
202-879-4400
online@aft.org
http://www.aft.org

The AFT is a professional membership organization for teachers (including art teachers) at all levels. In addition to membership benefits, the federation offers information on important issues affecting educators, salary surveys, and useful periodicals.

American Institute for
Conservation of Historic
and Artistic Works

1717 K Street, NW, Suite 200
Washington, DC 20006
202-452-9545
info@aic-faic.org
http://aic.stanford.edu

This organization offers information on student membership and art conservation careers and education, including useful online publications such as *Conservation Training in the United States* and *Undergraduate Prerequisites for Admission into Graduate Conservation Training Programs.* Its site also features a variety of useful resources about caring for art and selecting a conservator.

American Institute of
Graphic Arts

164 Fifth Avenue
New York, NY 10010
212-807-1990
http://www.aiga.org

This professional association for graphic designers and related professionals is dedicated to the promotion of excellence in the field of design through publications, exhibitions, competitions, seminars, conferences, and student membership. Visit the Ideas for Students section at its Web site to read *Graphic Design: A Career Guide,* which covers educational and career requirements. The section also offers tips on presenting your portfolio and avoiding resume mistakes.

American Psychological
Association (APA)

750 First Street, NE
Washington, DC 20002-4242
800-374-2721
http://www.apa.org

The APA offers a variety of useful information for students who are interested in pursuing careers in psychology-related fields (including art therapy). Visit its Web site to read publications such as *Psychology as a Career* and titles from its

Psychology Education and Careers Guidebook Series. There is also information on earnings, scholarships, and student membership for graduate students.

American Society of Media Photographers (ASMP)

150 North Second Street
Philadelphia, PA 19106
215-451-2767
http://www.asmp.org

The ASMP promotes the rights of photographers, educates its members in business practices, and promotes high standards of ethics.

Antique and Collectible Associations (ACA)

PO Box 4389
Davidson, NC 28036
800-287-7127
info@antiqueandcollectible.com
http://www.antiqueandcollectible.com

Contact the ACA for industry information, a list of online art galleries, and appraisal information.

Art Dealers Association of America

575 Madison Avenue
New York, NY 10022
212-940-8590
http://www.artdealers.org

Contact this association for art resources and listings of galleries.

ArtNetwork

PO Box 1360
Nevada City, CA 95959

800-383-0677
info@artmarketing.com
http://www.artmarketing.com

This organization helps artists market and sell their art. It offers marketing tools, a newsletter, a directory of artists, and reference resources.

Appraisers Association of America

386 Park Avenue South, Suite 2000
New York, NY 10016
212-889-5404
appraisers@appraisersassoc.org
http://www.appraisersassoc.org

Contact this organization for information on student membership and the Augustus H. Fisher Fellowship.

College Art Association

275 Seventh Avenue
New York, NY 10001
212-691-1051
nyoffice@collegeart.org
http://www.collegeart.org

The CAA is a professional membership organization for art teachers and researchers. Contact it for information on graduate fellowships.

Fine Art Dealers Association (FADA)

PO Box D1
Carmel, CA 93921
http://www.fada.com

Contact the FADA for information on art galleries nationwide and special events.

Graphic Artists Guild
90 John Street, Suite 403
New York, NY 10038-3202
212-791-3400
http://www.gag.org

This organization promotes and protects the economic interests of members and is committed to improving conditions for all creators of graphic art and to raising standards for the entire industry. It is a union that embraces creators at all levels of skill and expertise who produce graphic art intended for presentation as originals or reproductions. The organization is committed to improving conditions for all creators of graphic art and to raising standards for the entire industry.

Guild of Natural Science Illustrators
PO Box 652
Ben Franklin Station
Washington, DC 20044-0652
301-309-1514
gnsihome@his.com
http://www.gnsi.org

The guild sells inexpensive publications for aspiring natural science illustrators, such as *Careers in Scientific Illustration* and *Scientific Illustration Courses and Books.*

International Sculpture Center (ISC)
14 Fairgrounds Road, Suite B
Hamilton, NJ 08619-3447
609-689-1051
isc@sculpture.org
http://www.sculpture.org

Visit the center's Web site for a searchable database of undergraduate and graduate sculpture programs, profiles of famous sculptors, a message board, and a searchable online directory of selected works and credentials of ISC member sculptors. Student sculptors can post a mini portfolio at the site for free. Contact the ISC for more information.

International Society of Appraisers
1131 Seventh Street, SW, Suite 105
Renton, WA 98055
206-241-0359
isa@isa-appraisers.org
http://www.isa-appraisers.org

Contact the society for information about appraising and continuing education.

National Art Education Association
1916 Association Drive
Reston, VA 20191-1590
703-860-8000
http://www.naea-reston.org

Contact the association for information on student membership and useful publications.

National Art Materials Trade Association (NAMTA)
15806 Brookway Drive, Suite 300
Huntersville, NC 28078
704-892-6244
http://www.namta.org

NAMTA represents art material retailers and suppliers. Contact the association for information on scholarships and job listings.

National Assembly of State Arts Agencies

1029 Vermont Avenue, NW,
  Second Floor
Washington, DC 20005
202-347-6352
nasaa@nasaa-arts.org
http://www.nasaa-arts.org

This association supports established and emerging artists and arts organizations. For information on art programs, contact your state agency or the assembly.

National Association of Schools of Art and Design (NASAD)

11250 Roger Bacon Drive, Suite 21
Reston, VA 20190-5248
703-437-0700
info@arts-accredit.org
http://nasad.arts-accredit.org

Contact the NASAD for information on accredited arts programs. You can search a free online version of its list of accredited institutions by name, city, and/or state. (For a small fee, you can search a more extensive version of the list.) Additionally, visit the FAQ: Students, Parents, Public section for useful information on preparing to study art or design in college, applying for financial aid, and accreditation.

National Coalition of Arts Therapies Associations (NCATA)

8455 Colesville Road, Suite 1000
Silver Spring, MD 20910
http://www.nccata.org

Visit the NCATA Web site for a detailed overview of all the forms of creative arts therapy.

National Council for Accreditation of Teacher Education

2010 Massachusetts Avenue, NW,
  Suite 500
Washington, DC 20036
202-466-7496
ncate@ncate.org
http://www.ncate.org

Visit the council's Web site to read the following resources: FAQs about Careers in Education, What to Look for in a Teacher Preparation Program, and Why Attend an NCATE Accredited College of Education?

National Council on Education for the Ceramic Arts

77 Erie Village Square, Suite 280
Erie, CO 80516-6996
866-266-2322
office@nceca.net
http://www.nceca.net

Contact the council for information on student membership, conferences, fellowships, and a list of U.S. programs offering degrees in ceramics.

National Endowment for the Arts (NEA)

1100 Pennsylvania Avenue, NW
Washington, DC 20506
202-682-5400
http://arts.endow.gov

Congress established the NEA in 1965 to support excellence in the arts. It offers grants to artists and arts organizations, as well as various community-based programs. Visit its Web site for more information.

National Press Photographers Association (NPPA)
3200 Croasdaile Drive, Suite 306
Durham, NC 27705
919-383-7246
info@nppa.org
http://www.nppa.org

The NPPA maintains a job bank, provides educational and career information, and makes insurance available to its members. It also publishes *News Photographer* magazine.

National Sculpture Society (NSS)
237 Park Avenue
New York, NY 10017
212-764-5645
http://www.sculpturereview.com/nss.html

The NSS is the oldest organization of professional sculptors in the United States. Contact it for information on membership, scholarships, and competitions. You can also view the work of members at its Web site.

Professional Photographers of America
229 Peachtree Street, NE, Suite 2200
Atlanta, GA 30303
800-786-6277
csc@ppa.com
http://www.ppa.com

Contact this organization for information on certification, training, competitions, and *Professional Photographer* magazine.

Sculptors Guild
110 Greene Street, Suite 601
New York, NY 10012
212-431-5669
http://www.sculptorsguild.org

This is a nonprofit organization of professional sculptors. Visit its Web site to view samples of works created by its members.

Society of Children's Book Writers and Illustrators
8271 Beverly Boulevard
Los Angeles, CA 90048
323-782-1010
scbwi@scbwi.org
http://www.scbwi.org

Visit the society's Web site for detailed information on the marketplace for children's book writers and illustrators.

Society of Illustrators
128 East 63rd Street
New York, NY 10021-7303
212-838-2560
info@societyillustrators.org
http://www.societyillustrators.org

This national institution promotes and stimulates interest in the art of illustration by offering exhibits, lectures, educational programs, and social exchange. Contact the society for information on student membership, career information, and a list of postsecondary art schools that offer courses, continuing education, or majors in the applied arts of illustration, cartooning, graphic design, or visual communications.

Student Photographic Society

229 Peachtree Street, NE, Suite 2200
Atlanta, GA 30303
866-886-5325
http://www.studentphoto.com

Contact the society for information on student membership, careers, and competitions.

World Studio Foundation

200 Varick Street, Suite 507
New York, NY 10014
http://www.worldstudio.org

This foundation has a special commitment to issues of social awareness, the environment, and diversity. To further these goals, it offers scholarships for high school seniors and college students and mentoring programs for inner-city artists ages 14 to 20. Although the foundation focuses its programs on underrepresented minorities, all are eligible to apply for its scholarships and participate in its programs. Contact the foundation for more information.

Index

Entries and page numbers in **bold** indicate major treatment of a topic.

A